Paradigms
of Jouissance

Psychoanalytical Notebooks

London Society
of the New
Lacanian School

Issue 34, December 2019

Director of NLS Publications: Bernard Seynhaeve
Consulting Editor: Pierre-Gilles Guéguen
Editor in Chief: Janet Haney
Assistant Editor: Roger Litten
Cover Image: Alasdair Duncan
Text setting & cover design: Linda Lundin
Translators: Thelma Sowley, Michele Julien,
Janet Haney, Alasdair Duncan
Proofing: John Haney
Secretary: Sophia Berouka

Published by the London Society of the NLS
Correspondence Address:
Psychoanalytical Notebooks, 42D Maple Street, London W1T 6HF
Email: janetrhaney@gmail.com

ISBN 978-1-9161576-1-3

Contents

Janet Haney and Roger Litten   5
— *Editorial*

Three interventions by Jacques-Alain Miller

— *Six Paradigms of Jouissance*   11

— *Milanese Intuitions*   81

— *A Fantasy*   139

Editorial

Jacques-Alain Miller's encounter with Jacques Lacan has had a definitive role in shaping the reception of Lacan's work within psychoanalysis and beyond. It led Lacan to leave the legacy of his work in Miller's hands, nominating him as "the one who knows how to read me". Miller, in turn, has dedicated a lifetime to securing the legacy of Lacan's work via the establishing of Lacan's seminar in written form and via his own course at the University of Paris VIII, the Lacanian Orientation, teaching various generations how to read Lacan.

Lacan's seminar, delivered over three decades, essentially asked: How does psychoanalysis work? What are its means, its goals, its conditions? How are these to be rethought in the instance of each patient, each analyst, and, most importantly, in the light of the changes in the discursive framework within which psychoanalysis is practised?

Like Lacan's teaching, psychoanalysis is neither a doctrine nor a fixed technique. It might rather be considered a work of investigation that faces up to the challenges of a clinic inflected by modifications and reconfigurations of the discourses that shape the suffering of contemporary subjects and the demands that are addressed to us as practitioners. Lacanian psychoanalysis has shown itself to be eminently sensitive to these modifications, not simply in foregrounding the role of speech, language and discourse, but also in terms of the introduction of the concepts of jouissance, *objet petit a*, and the real, which constitute Lacan's particular contribution to the conceptualisation of what is at stake in psychoanalytic practice. He has given us the conceptual and clinical tools for reading the changes in the contemporary discourses along with the modifications in subjective and symptomatic positions that accompany them. In this way, Lacanian psychoanalysis has demonstrated its capacity to engage with the specific clinical challenges of our times.

No one has contributed more to bringing Lacan's work into alignment with these challenges than Jacques-Alain Miller. The three texts compiled in this issue of the *Psychoanalytical Notebooks*, selected from Miller's copious interventions on Lacan's teaching, provide us with snapshots of Miller's own trajectory through these questions. *Six Paradigms of Jouissance* helps us locate the core question in both the theory and the clinic, that of the relation between signifier and jouissance. Miller shows us how the different phases of that teaching can be grasped as ways of elaborating the implications of this pivotal question for psychoanalytic practice. The two subsequent texts, *Milanese Intuitions* and *A Fantasy*, then provide us with an indication of how some of these questions can be pursued in a demonstration of how Lacan's work meets up with the horizon of the subjectivity of our times, requiring a profound reconceptualisation of psychoanalytic practice today.

Each of these texts is the transcription of a spoken intervention that still bears the traces of the moment of its enunciation. Brought together here in revised and updated translation this small series of texts should suffice to give an indication to any reader who wishes to acquaint themselves with the contemporary Lacanian orientation why today in order to be Lacanian it is necessary to be Millerian.

But this is something that we leave to you the reader to decide.

Janet Haney and Roger Litten
December 2019

Six Paradigms of Jouissance

Jacques-Alain Miller

Six Paradigms of Jouissance
Jacques-Alain Miller

The six paradigms of jouissance in Lacan, as I presented them in Los Angeles, are simplified snapshots. They are plotted in an attempt to recreate, through their rapid superimposition, the movement which is the driving force that we see in Lacan's teaching on the doctrine of jouissance.

Paradigm 1: The 'Imaginarisation' of Jouissance
The first paradigm is that of the 'imaginarisation' of jouissance. Under this title, I describe the results of the first movement in Lacan's teaching on jouissance, which develops from the introduction

These three lessons were delivered as part of the course of J.-A.,Miller: Orientation lacanienne, III-1, "L'expérience du réel dans la cure analytique", (24, 31, March and 7 April 1999). This teaching took place under the auspices of the Department of Psychoanalysis at the University of Paris VIII. As Miller says at the outset, these lectures were themselves based on a series of lectures given in Los Angeles shortly before. Those lectures must surely have been given in English, but no record of them seems to be available. The current text has been translated from the French text which appeared in *La Cause freudienne*, No. 43, October 1999, pp. 7-29, which was established by Catherine Bonningue and published with the authorisation of J.-A. Miller. A previous English translation was published in *Lacanian Ink*, No. 17 as "Paradigms of Jouissance", translated by Jorge Jauregui, 2000. We thought it was time to celebrate the text with a new translation.

of the symbolic as forming a distinct dimension of analytic experience and its own order of existence.

These consequences regarding jouissance remain hidden as long as what primarily occupies the conceptual scene is the demonstration of the function of speech in the provision of meaning and of the field of language that supports it in its structure, and of the operations of history, that is, the retroactive dynamic of the subjectivations, the re-subjectivations, of facts and events. What dominates this first conceptual moment is communication conceived as intersubjective and dialectical.

This introductory Lacan was in place for such a long time, that it is imagined to be the base, the kernel, and even the sum total of his teaching.

What I call here 'communication' first takes the form of displaying in analytic experience the fundamental structural character of the relation of subject to subject, as Lacan explains in his "Intervention on Transference", where he himself calls what is going on the "dialectic of intersubjectivity".[1]

This intersubjectivity is of course corrected by the asymmetry which Lacan introduces progressively into the subject-to-subject relation. The

---

1 Lacan, J., "Presentation on Transference" given at 1951 Congress of "Romance Language-Speaking Psychoanalysts", transl. B. Fink, *Écrits*, London/New York, Norton, 2006, pp. 176-185. See also "Intervention on Transference" transl. J. Rose, in *Feminine Sexuality*, ed J. Mitchell and J. Rose, London, Macmillan, 1982, pp. 61-73.

two subjects are not equivalent in function, since it is the analyst-subject who mainly listens, punctuates, interprets, and through this decides the meaning. From this follows the introduction into communication of the agency of the big Other, even the absolute Other, a position with properties distinct from those of the subject who does not find there his identical correlate. A little later in Lacan's teaching, this Other takes the place of speech, of language, of structure, and the place of all determinations of the subject.

This is, briefly summarised, what appears to be the essential contribution, the innovation introduced by Lacan. This relation is inscribed on the symbolic axis, which we will write thus, and which ends this period:

$$A \rightarrow S$$

This moment, which has a certain duration in Lacan's teaching, shows that the conceptualisation in question remains fundamentally equivocal. It is always inscribed between two poles, those of speech and of language. On the side of speech, Lacan readily develops intersubjectivity, ever subject to revision. On the side of language he stresses, ever more so, the autonomy of the symbolic, the fact that the signifying chain, as it runs in the Other, has its own requirements, a logic.

This first elaboration is made to take account of what of the unconscious can be deciphered during the analytic experience. This is the aim of this construction. The initial ambiguity is there as well. In these first years of Lacan's teaching, the unconscious appears sometimes as language, and sometimes as speech. Sometimes the accent is put on the structure which it comprises, sometimes on the discourse that it emits, that it constitutes, to the point that the unconscious could be described by Lacan as a subject.

What is the effect of this introductory Lacan on the Freudian corpus? It has the effect of a caesura, as Lacan indicates on page 261 of the *Écrits*,[2] that of a separation produced in the Freudian corpus between that which marks the technique of deciphering the unconscious, which justifies this extraordinary assembly of communication and structure, and, on the other hand, the theory of instincts, indeed drives. Lacan emphasises deciphering in so far as it depends on the symbolic, that it presupposes therefore the difference between signifier and signified, and finds its place in a structure of communication.

Whence the question of what Freud comes to call the economic perspective, that is, the point

2 Lacan, J., "The Function and Field of Speech and Language in Psychoanalysis", transl. B. Fink, *Écrits*, NY/London Norton, 2006, p. 217.

of view of satisfaction. Something undoubtedly ciphers itself and deciphers itself in the formations of the unconscious. Freud has given us evidence of this. But also, for Freud, something is satisfied in this ciphering and deciphering. Lacan's response, conditioned by his emphasis on symbolic deciphering, is that the essential satisfaction is to be found within communication itself, that which derives from the liberation of meaning. In *Seminar V*, Lacan devotes himself to showing the special satisfaction which is attached to the fact that the Other endorses, admits the curious, surprising, and sometimes deviant linguistic formations that can come from the subject. This accord, which eventually translates into laughter when it comes to a joke, is all of a piece with whatever constitutes a satisfaction in the semantic order.

This satisfaction can be illustrated as much on the side of the subject as on the side of the Other. On the side of the subject, it is the imprisonment of meaning that causes suffering. Lacan thus describes the symptom, as a meaning not delivered. This imprisonment in structure is the translation of repression. The symptom maintains itself as repressed meaning – when Lacan played with the term 'consciousness', he even said 'repressed by the consciousness of the subject' – and satisfaction comes with the reappearance of the meaning. On the side of the Other, it is the reception, the registering, the validation of subjective meaning that culminates in recognition. If Lacan at that time emphasised the theme of recognition in such a way as to make the desire for recognition the most fundamental desire of the subject, it is in so far as this recognition brings satisfaction in the order of communication.

What happens to the economic point of view in this construction? The first answer is that it is symbolic satisfaction. But that does not cover everything that is there in Freud. Where are the drives, libidinal investment and its fixations, fantasy, the superego as well as the ego? This objection meets the response that the symbolic is not everything, that it leaves out of itself the imaginary, which is another order of reality whereby another order of satisfaction is accomplished. To put it another way, in front of symbolic satisfaction, which extends its empire throughout the psyche, stands imaginary satisfaction, which we will properly call jouissance.

In this first Lacanian paradigm, the libido has imaginary status, and jouissance as imaginary does not come from language, speech and communication. It does not come from the subject, strictly speaking. It comes from the ego as an imaginary instance – and Lacan interprets the ego on the basis of narcissism, and narcissism on the basis of the mirror stage. He finds here, quite naturally, the Freudian formula of the ego as a reservoir of libido, and goes as far as to say, on p. 427 of the *Écrits*, "by which narcissism envelops the forms of desire."[3]

If we have to look for the place of jouissance as distinct from symbolic satisfaction, we find it on the imaginary axis a — a' where Lacan tries to put everything that Freud called libidinal investment. We see Lacan going through Freud's work and describing everything as imaginary that cannot be ranked as symbolic satisfaction.

Jouissance strictly speaking – imaginary jouissance – is not intersubjective but intra-imaginary. It is not dialectical, but is constantly described by Lacan as permanent, stagnant and inert. Even before his Rome report,[4] transference is considered not as belonging to the dialectic of the analytic experience but, on the contrary, as falling within the imaginary dimension, as appearing in a moment of stagnation in the dialectic, and as reproducing what Lacan calls the permanent modes of object constitution. In the same way, in the "Seminar on the Purloined Letter",[5] imaginary factors are characterised by their inertia and are considered as being only the shadows and reflections of what is achieved in the symbolic dialectic.

3 Lacan, J., "The Freudian Thing", *Écrits, op. cit.*, p. 355
4 Lacan, J., "The Function and Field of Speech and Language in Psychoanalysis", *Écrits, op. cit.,* pp. 197-268.
5 Lacan, J., "Seminar on 'The Purloined Letter'" *Écrits, op. cit.*, pp. 6-48.

This first paradigm stresses the disjunction between signifier and jouissance. What has rightly been understood as the period of the separation of the field of the ego from the field of the unconscious, once we recognise it, is in fact the basic disjunction of signifier and jouissance. The signifier has its logic, its course, and as such is distinct, separated from its attachment to jouissance. This imaginary jouissance is thus susceptible to a certain number of emergences in the analytic experience – when a fault manifests itself, a rupture in the symbolic chain.

There is a whole part of the Lacanian clinic which consists of reporting several phenomena of ruptures of the symbolic chain, and to the occurrences of imaginary jouissance. Thus, his reading of the 'acting out',[6] taken from the case of Ernst Kris, tells of the emergence of a primordially entrenched oral relation, that is to say, of an element of imaginary jouissance. Or again, *Seminar IV*[7] repeatedly tries to show the appearance of transient perversions in the experience which are regularly considered as occurrences of imaginary jouissance there where the symbolic elaboration is lacking or fails. It is again in the same paradigm, that we find the formulation where Lacan first

6 Lacan, J., e.g, "The Direction of the Treatments and the Principles of its Power" *Écrits*, p. 510
7 Lacan, J., *Le Séminaire*, livre IV, *La relation d'objet* (1956-57), Paris, Seuil, 1994.

presents the superego as obscene and ferocious. The superego is, for him, that which emerges from such a symbolic failure and gives form to imaginary jouissance.

In general, it is when the symbolic chain breaks that the objects, products and effects of jouissance arise from the imaginary. Everything that in Freud is, strictly speaking, libidinal is ascribed to imaginary jouissance as an obstacle, as a barrier. This is why Lacan presents the axis of imaginary jouissance as crossing the symbolic axis, as an obstacle or barrier to symbolic elaboration.

This first paradigm is not without ambiguity since, from one aspect, the imaginary is clearly that which remains outside the grasp of the symbolic whilst, from another aspect, Lacan always adds that this imaginary is at the same time dominated by the symbolic. We have then in his writings and in his seminars a tension between that which maintains an 'autonomy of the imaginary', which has its own properties, its own source distinct from language and speech, and at the same time a more muted note of domination of the imaginary by the symbolic, a refrain that swells, obtrudes and becomes dominant.

It is a timely reminder, indeed, that, in Lacan, the imaginary serves as material for the symbolic, that, in particular, it serves as material for the symptom, it is inserted into the symbolic so that the symbolic acts upon it. But at the beginning of his teaching we only find this in the form of very general propositions. All the detail is devoted to the signifying chain and to its autonomy, whilst, as if in reserve, it is noted that imaginary elements are susceptible to symbolic recuperation. This extraordinary operation performed on Freud's text – the imaginarisation of jouissance – thus finds itself accompanied by, and progressively displaced by, outclassed by, the transposition of the imaginary into the symbolic.

Lacan's initial move, as liberator, was accomplished under the banner of the non-rapport between the imaginary and the symbolic. He extricated, in unforgettable fashion, the symbolic order in its autonomy, and taught analysts that there was something like logic, independent of all reference to the jouissance of the body, to establish its laws, to answer to the principles, and also to condition everything that any one of us can say. This watchword about the purity of the symbolic can say only one thing – its non-rapport with the imaginary as the place which in Freud is called 'libido'.

Paradigm 2: The Significantisation of Jouissance

The second paradigm is that of the significantisation of jouissance. It is the second move in Lacan's teaching. It does not simply succeed the first chronologically. It mixes with it, completes it, and then progressively asserts itself. It takes over the first paradigm and finally dominates it entirely.

We witness a true conceptual re-writing which tries to demonstrate that all the terms that have fallen into the imaginary category are, in the final analysis, so well incorporated into the symbolic that they are fundamentally symbolic terms.

The first paradigm sets up this huge reserve of the imaginary and, then, in a second move, Lacan shows the consistency and the symbolic articulation of what is imaginary. For example, at first transference is related to imaginary jouissance, and then, in a second moment, finds itself displaced onto the symbolic axis.

Not only are the drives structured in terms of language – Lacan begins to detach the drives from jouissance, which is merely imaginary – they are capable of metonymy, substitution, and combination, but the drive is written on the basis of the symbolic subject, of the demand, that is to say an eminently symbolic term. This formulation $(S \lozenge D)$ is a key moment in the significantisation of jouissance. Lacan inscribes this demand of the Other in the very formula for the drive, that is to say he retranscribes the drive in symbolic terms.

This is also what happens in the case of the fantasy. In the first paradigm, the fantasy is eminently the connection which links a to a' in a transitivity that requires, moreover, the Name of the Father to impose here the order which is superimposed. And in *Seminar V*, we see fulfilled the displacement of the concept of transference from the imaginary register to that of the symbolic.

Lacan tries to show that there is no fantasy that is not also a scenario, and then that there is no fantasy that is not assimilable to a signifying chain, whence the formula for fantasy which is taken from this second paradigm ($S \Diamond a$), where the image in its signifying function is articulated to the symbolic subject. This writing will remain for a very long time in Lacan's teaching as the symbol of the connection between the symbolic and the libidinal. It will even determine, for a very long time, the centring of the treatment on the fantasy as being, par excellence, the nodal point where the imaginary and the symbolic come together, as the essential quilting point for these two registers.

The displacement of the concept of regression from the imaginary register to that of the symbolic is inscribed in the same movement. Regression, which is related in the first paradigm to a disintegration, a deconstruction of the ego and its imaginary relations, is, on the contrary, shown to be symbolic in nature, that is to say that it realises itself through the return of signifiers that have been used in previous demands.

The big moment of this paradigm is the moment when the phallus, whose status as image already distinguishes it from the organ, is displaced in order to privilege its symbolic status. We notice it continuously in *Seminar V*, since, after his work on "A question prior to...",[8] where the phallus appears as imaginary, we see Lacan shifting his orientation until he arrives at the phallus as signifier. If we compare the formulae, term by term, we see only a contradiction, whereas the term 'phallic' is dragged into this significantisation of imaginary jouissance which Lacan is applying very systematically to all the terms.

This culminates in the general demonstration that the libido itself is written into the signifier – as he does in his sixth seminar, even if it is already present in his fifth. He pushes the significantisation of jouissance so far that he shows it to be equivalent to the signified of an unconscious signifying chain whose vocabulary would be constituted by the drive. It is this that Lacan called 'desire'.

There again, this was unprecedented, since it is in this concept of desire that the significantisation of jouissance is achieved, is realised, is carried out. It is clearly a mortified jouissance, a jouissance that has passed to the signifier. It is the jouissance of the kind that features on the upper level of Lacan's great graph, where we have

8 Lacan, J., "On a Question Prior to Any Possible Treatment of Psychosis", *Écrits, op. cit.* pp. 445-488.

the trajectory from jouissance to castration that achieves this significantisation.

Once again, we can ask: where is satisfaction? Answer: it is the satisfaction of desire. Lacan spells out the modes of satisfaction that are attached to the signifiers of desire: to have close to oneself a person, a function, an authority that represents the signifier of desire.

There is yet another satisfaction, which holds to desire this time in the same way as the signified runs under the signifier. It is the pure satisfaction of metonymy. Whence comes the notion of undoing those identifications, and especially phallic identification, that would hinder the free course of desire. This doesn't go beyond what is there in Freud, because it does not give the answer to: what is the true satisfaction of the drive? It can't give the answer, because the drive is reduced there to a signifying chain. Thus, anything one can say about satisfaction is always said in symbolic terms.

It is essentially the effacement of jouissance by the signifier that appears in this paradigm, which is determined by the model of erasure, which highlights the effect of sublimation, the *Aufhebung*. It is this that is repeated in the line which goes from jouissance to castration in the graph of desire. The signifier annuls jouissance and returns it to you in the form of signified desire.

In relation to the previous paradigm, this paradigm responds to an inverse movement of the absorption of jouissance into the symbolic, with the imaginary continuing to exist in its own dimension. It is in this movement that we see the great Lacanian invention of the mathemes. We suddenly see the minus phi of the phallic image symbolised and subtracted. We see the emergence of capital phi of the signifier of desire, later signifier of jouissance, and also the matheme of the fantasy – imaginary term resituated in the symbolic – the matheme of the drive, etc. All these terms are enshrined in their place in Lacan's graph.

Where is jouissance then? It is essentially distributed between the two terms of desire and fantasy. On the one hand, it is desire, that is to say signified by the unconscious demand. It seems justified in this respect to write it thus: the drive as unconscious demand in the position of the signifier and desire in the position of the signified.

$$\frac{S}{s} \rightarrow \frac{(\mathcal{S} \lozenge D)}{d}$$

Jouissance in one respect is nothing other than desire, which is at the same time dead desire. This makes all the more important the second term where Lacan inscribes jouissance, that is, the fantasy which accounts for everything that jouissance has of life. The fantasy consists of life, the living body, by the insertion of *petit a* as an image included in a signifying structure, an image of jouissance captured in the symbolic. This *petit a* retains all its imaginary contours and focuses the very spot where libido is linked to the living body. On the other hand, with the barred subject, we have by contrast a deathly being because it is merely a signifying function.

Paradigm 3: Impossible Jouissance

Pushing this significantisation of jouissance to its limit introduces the necessity of a third paradigm, that is to say, the necessity of the extension, the correction, the addition of the distinct paradigm introduced by the seminar on *The Ethics of Psychoanalysis*, and which we can call that of impossible jouissance, which means real jouissance. Lacan himself indicated that this seminar made for him a kind of cut. It constitutes a privileged reference point in that it is the third attribution of jouissance in Lacan, jouissance attributed to the real.

This is what is meant by *das Ding*, which Lacan highlighted in Freud's text as a sort of *Witz*. It is a term that is not constituted like Lacan's mathemes. Its strange – *unheimlich* – character shows that it is not a question of a symbolic term.

What then is meant by *das Ding*, the Thing? It signifies that satisfaction, the true drive satisfaction, the *Befriedigung*, is found neither in the imaginary nor the symbolic, that it is outside what is symbolised, that it is of the order of the real. This means that the symbolic order, like the imaginary relation – that is to say, everything in the two-level assembly of Lacan's great graph – is set up against real jouissance in order to contain real jouissance.

This is a fundamental redrawing of the graph implying a substitution of defence for repression. Repression is a concept that belongs to the symbolic and conditions the very notion of decipherment, whereas defence indicates a fundamental orientation of being. As Lacan says, defence already exists even before the conditions of repression as such are formulated.

In *The Ethics of Psychoanalysis*, we are targeting a zone exterior to this montage, one that in some way determines it. It is also a question of a barrier, but not the barrier of the imaginary. It is the barrier that the real opposes as much to the imaginary as to the symbolic.

Lacan describes two other barriers which adjoin this essential real barrier: the symbolic barrier – that of the law, that which says, you must not, you cannot – and then the imaginary barrier which he describes in the case of Antigone under the form of the appearance of the beautiful preventing the

Jacques-Alain Miller

attainment of the Thing, before crossing over in the direction of the Thing. There is a symbolic barrier, there is an imaginary barrier, but these are conditioned by this withdrawal of the Thing beyond symbolisation.

The discontinuity is much more marked in this paradigm than that between the first two which are mixed up in Lacan's texts. Here we have a true break. Jouissance passes to the real. It expresses itself, is described as 'off the grid', and is distinguished by a character that is absolute. This allows Lacan to develop a whole system of substitution of terms which can come into this place.

This paradigm is no longer bound to a model of erasure of jouissance by the signifier which is open to an *Aufhebung*, but to that of the vase, which Lacan borrows from Heidegger. The vase is a created object which is added to the world. It has at the same time, paradoxically, the property of introducing an absence, and in this way the possibility of filling it.

It is on this property that Lacan pinpoints the Thing as equivalent to the annulment that is castration. This marks in some way the reduction of jouissance to an empty space. That space can be, thereby, and in the same breath, equivalent to the barred subject. But this introduces in its turn the possibility of filling it, along with the notion of a supplement which will never be adequate.

It is here that the extraordinary litany of terms opens up, imaginary and symbolic elements, that Lacan gradually enumerates throughout his *Ethics*, and which are apt to come to this place. Any symbolic term is apt to come to this place if it is cut off from the rest of the system, if it is endowed with the property of absoluteness.

Lacan likes to show that Kant's moral law, which is a symbolic statement par excellence and which implies the annulment of all jouissance, is the reverse side of the Thing, of jouissance, but is at the same time identical to *das Ding*, because it has the same dumb, blind and absolute character. This term substitutes itself for the dumb reality of *das Ding* – dumb because it is outside the symbolic. The mother, who is the object par excellence, protected by the Oedipal barrier, comes to the place of *das Ding*. Science responds to the first demand of *das Ding*, because it is absolute, and because it comes to the same place. In a general way, a list of increasingly meaningless substitute objects is introduced. It is Jacques Prévert's matchbox, whose drawer is a variation on the model of the vase.

In this paradigm where jouissance is highlighted as outside systemisation, there is no access to jouissance other than by a forcing, that is to say it is structurally inaccessible, except by transgression. Hence the praise of heroic transgression and the tribe of heroes that begins to invade Lacan's

Seminar. It is, by the way, the great figure of Antigone who appears here in the first instance as crossing the barrier of the city, the law, the barrier of the beautiful, to advance into the zone of horror that jouissance implies. A heroism of jouissance which Lacan writes as a kind of *symphonie fantastique* that emerges of itself in having to renounce the purring of the symbolic and the imaginary in order to attain the tearing of jouissance.

This third paradigm puts a strong emphasis on a profound disjunction between the signifier and jouissance. It recalls something of the first paradigm, where we have the disjunction because jouissance is imaginary. We find here something of this disjunction because jouissance is real. Here is a kind of loop which we follow in Lacan's teaching.

We see clearly here the opposition between libido transcribed as desire, where it appears between the signifiers, and libido as *das Ding*, where it appears beyond signifier and signified. I add that in this paradigm the opposition between pleasure and jouissance is essential. The pleasure principle appears in some way as a natural barrier to jouissance, and thus the opposition is established between the homeostasis of pleasure and the excesses constitutive of jouissance. It is at the same time the opposition between that which is of the order of the good – on the side of pleasure – and that which carries the 'always bad' that is jouissance. Which is why Lacan, in his Seminar, summons up Sadean jouissance as the epitome of this paradigm. It is also an opposition between, on the one side, that which deceives – pleasure, the signifier, the imaginary and the semblant – and, on the other side, that which is real.

This raises a small difficulty when the unconscious is defined as structured like a language, as the discourse of the Other, to the extent that the unconscious does not include this jouissance which is beyond symbolisation. It is, in a way, that which cannot be spoken. That is why Lacan can say, on page 90 of *The Ethics*, that at the level of the unconscious the subject lies about *das Ding*, that there is a sort of original lie about jouissance which is the theme of this disjunction, a fundamental separation between signifier and jouissance.

What Freud called defence is the original lie itself, the structural lie which the subject sustains in the space of jouissance. Lacan doesn't really develop this in this seminar on *The Ethics*, but the symptom, which he had spoken about until then as repression, is there related to defence. He brings the symptom back to the structurally disharmonious character of the relation to jouissance. The symptom is the way in which the subject formulates that jouissance is bad. In other words, the symptom establishes itself exactly on the barrier between signifier and jouissance, and it echoes the basic disharmony of jouissance with the subject.

In the second paradigm jouissance is taken up in the Other, jouissance in the symbolic is reduced to desire and the fantasy. This third paradigm, elaborated in *The Ethics of Psychoanalysis*, consists in taking note of what of jouissance is not covered by desire and fantasy. It is therefore obliged to put jouissance beyond the symbolic and the imaginary and into the real. This paradigm puts jouissance on the side of the Thing.

What, ultimately, is the Thing? As a term, it is the Other of the Other. It is that which, in respect to the signifying system of the Other, swollen with what has been translated from the imaginary, is the Other. It does not have the signifying structure of the Other, it is the Other of the Other precisely in terms of what is lacking in the Other. The value that Lacan recognises here in jouissance as the Thing is equivalent to the barred Other. It is this that makes jouissance the Other of the Other, in the sense of that which lacks, of that which lacks in the Other:

$$J = \cancel{A}$$

In one sense it is an impasse to isolate the Thing as beyond symbolisation, the same impasse as that produced by Lacan's inaugural gesture. Lacan will put this impasse to work in the following seminars, where he will try to think through the relation between the signifier and that which is beyond symbolisation. How does he do it? He does it by making jouissance, which emerges here under the forms of the Thing, beyond symbolisation, appear from now on as object. The development of the *object a* that follows is the precise response to this. There is no chance of forming a new alliance between jouissance and the Other if we don't go beyond the Thing as massive jouissance.

Paradigm 4: Normal Jouissance

In Los Angeles I cautiously called the fourth paradigm, which I refer to *Seminar XI*, 'fragmented jouissance', but now I think I can go as far as calling it 'normal jouissance'.

There is an extraordinary antithesis between *The Ethics of Psychoanalysis* and *The Four Fundamental Concepts of Psychoanalysis*, in which Lacan poses a new alliance between the symbolic and jouissance.

Throughout *The Ethics of Psychoanalysis*, we have a demonstration of the massive character of jouissance, situated in a place that is usually out of reach, and which demands a transgression, a forcing, into an unfathomable space that can only be reached through transgression. In the seminar on *The Four Concepts* we have a jouissance fragmented into *objets petit a*. It is not situated in an abyss, but in a little hollow. Lacan says that the *objet petit a* is simply the presence of a hollow, an empty space. Jouissance is not reached by heroic transgression, as in the third paradigm, but by a circuit of the drive, by a drive which makes a round trip.

The *Stimmung*, the affective colouration of the two seminars, is absolutely opposed. In *The Ethics of Psychoanalysis* we have jouissance linked to horror; it is necessary to pass through sadism to understand something of it. When one is in the place of jouissance, the experience is that of terrible bodily fragmentation – a single death is not enough to account for it, Lacan adds a second. In the seminar on *The Four Concepts* the model of the relation to jouissance is art, the picture, the peaceful contemplation of the art object. As Lacan says, the work of art soothes people, it reassures them, it makes them feel good.

We might speak of inverted trajectories. On the one side, in *The Ethics of Psychoanalysis*, we start with the pleasure principle, with homeostasis, all those symbols and images which are only there to serve the pleasure principle, and then, as the seminar progresses, we come to sadistic fragmentation. In *Seminar XI* we begin with the body fragmented by the partial drives, by erogenous zones which are autonomous and only think of their own good, and then by way of contrast, if there is an integration, it is achieved thanks to drive jouissance, which is an automatic jouissance achieved by following the normal path of the drive, its round trip, without transgression.

What is this change from one paradigm to the other? It is that Lacan in this fourth paradigm now denies the cleavage between the signifier and jouissance. He forges an alliance, a tight articulation between the signifier and jouissance. The seminar on *The Four Concepts* revises the very basis from which Lacan started in his Rome Discourse.

What is the purpose of the mechanism of alienation and separation, of all this paraphernalia that Lacan seeks in set theory? What is it all about? It is about a tight articulation of the symbolic with jouissance. It is about showing that jouissance is not an addition in its own right, that it inserts itself into the functioning of the signifier, that it is connected to the signifier.

Lacan distinguishes two operations, alienation and separation; separation responding to alienation. Why two operations? The first, alienation, is properly and even purely symbolic, and he tries to show that the result of this operation necessarily implies a response of jouissance. This is separation.

Let us try to make a conceptual analysis in Freudian terms of what Lacan calls alienation. This notion aims to unite the two concepts of identification and repression. First, identification implies a signifier that represents the subject, a signifier that is in some way absorbent, that is in the Other, with which the subject identifies itself whilst remaining, at the same time, an empty set. This is what Lacan calls the division of the subject.

On the one hand, the subject exists as an empty set, and is represented as a signifier. On the other hand, it simultaneously meets repression. If we take a signifying chain, of which the minimum is S_1-S_2, repression says that one of the two goes under, the one that represents the subject.

What Lacan calls separation is his way of retranslating the function of the drive as responding to identification and repression. Where the empty subject was, there comes the lost object, the *objet petit a*. Whereas, in *The Ethics*, we need a terrible transgression in order to reach jouissance, here separation implies the normal functioning of the drive in as much as it responds to the void that results from identification and repression. It implies a superimposition of the structure of the subject onto that of jouissance. And, in the same way, given that the subject is a lack-of-being, the definition of the drive includes a gap or a small hollow.

Have you noticed that, at the beginning of the seminar on *The Four Concepts*, Lacan describes the unconscious as he has never done before?

Everyone swallowed this because it was so well argued. Ever since his first paradigm, Lacan had always described the unconscious rather as an order, a chain, a regularity, and here at the beginning of *The Four Concepts* he re-centres all the unconscious on a discontinuity, and not just the discontinuity that is compatible with a signifying order. He describes the unconscious precisely as a rim that opens and closes.

Why choose to emphasise that which opens and closes? The answer is clear. It is to make the unconscious equivalent to an erogenous zone. He describes the unconscious precisely as an anus or as a mouth. He describes it on the model of an erogenous zone to show that there is here a structural commonality between the symbolic unconscious and the function of the drive. It is because he begins in this way that he allows himself to say, in a phrase which is the key phrase of the Seminar, page 165 – *Something in the apparatus of the body is structured in the same way as the unconscious.*[9]

His procedure is very different. He has structured the unconscious in the same way as something in the bodily apparatus, like that of an

9 Lacan, J., *Seminar XI, The Four Fundamental Concepts of Psychoanalysis*, ed. J.-A. Miller, transl. A. Sheridan, London, Penguin Books, 1977, p. 181: "Well! It is in so far as something in the apparatus of the body is structured in the same way, it is because of the topological unity of the gaps in play, that the drive assumes its role in the functioning of the unconscious."

erogenous zone, as a rim that opens and closes. There he fashions jouissance onto the subject itself. This implies that he is introducing in miniature, and in the drive itself, the model of the vase. The hollow with which the drive is concerned is that which we have met as the Heideggerian vase in *The Ethics of Psychoanalysis*, the hollow created by signifying annulment which comes to find itself filled, inadequately every time, with an object. And in this paradigm, libido is that object.

The myth of the lamella, as Lacan has introduced it, is a new definition of libido, no longer as signified desire, no longer as *das Ding,* that massive jouissance beyond signification that is only reached by transgression, but libido as an organ, as lost object and the matrix for all lost objects. He calls *separation* the recuperation of libido as lost object. With his apparatus he tries to show that it responds to the signifying lack which follows from the articulation of identification and repression.

What causes some difficulty is that this lost object, at the point where Lacan brings it into his *Seminar XI*, is a loss which is independent of the signifier, a natural loss. This is what he introduces on page 847 of the *Écrits – Here this libido as lost object represents that part of living which gets lost in what happens in the paths of sex.*[10] He considers the fact that, like the amoeba, we are individualised and that sexed reproduction is equivalent to a loss of life.

In other words, this hole is introduced here as a loss, and proved to be a natural loss. This is Lacan's continual refrain. When he elaborated the mirror stage, for example, he referred it to the prematurity of birth, which is to say, again, a natural lack. There is here a dissymmetry, since on the one hand we have the signifying lack, the S̸, and then it is articulated to a natural lack, to that loss which occurs naturally.

There is, then, a new departure in this paradigm, since, with these two operations of alienation and separation, jouissance is, in some way, reformulated in a mechanism. Whilst all the stress of *The Ethics of Psychoanalysis* is put in its invariable place in relation to mechanisms, combinations, and slippages of the signifier and the fluctuations of the imaginary, *Seminar XI* constitutes a reprise of Lacan's fundamental ambition, which was laid down in the second paradigm. It is a reprise by other means of significantisation, taking account

10 Lacan, J., "Position of the Unconscious", *Écrits, op. cit.*, p. 718: "My lamella represents here the part of a living being that is lost when that being is produced through the straits of sex."

of the results of the researches and the elaboration of *Seminar VII*. Nevertheless, at the same time this constitutes a cut in relation to this initial ternary, to the extent that, instead of appearing irreducible to the symbolic, or instead of being entirely reduced to the signifier, jouissance is distinguished as such and at the same time inscribed upon the functioning of a system.

The conjunction of the two operations of alienation and separation implies a discreet substitution where we meet the difficulty intrinsic to this conjunction. This substitution is found in "Position of the Unconscious" in the *Écrits*. The operation of alienation only gives us the subject of the signifier reduced to a lack of signifier, that is, the subject has no other substance than the empty set. You can grope around for a substance able to experience jouissance, but you find nothing. To be able to present the operation of separation and the introduction of *objet petit a* as responding to the lack of a signifier, one must discreetly substitute the living body, the sexed body, for the subject. One must also introduce the properties of the sexed body, in particular its mortality, its relation to the Other sex, its individuality, and by the same token that which Lacan translates in the form of a loss of life that the existence of the body of the subject carries. One can then introduce the objects of the drive as repairing and filling in this loss of life. Jouissance is therefore distributed in the development of Lacan's teaching under the figure of the *objet petit a*, that is, something more modest, scaled down, more easily handled than the Thing. The *objet petit a*, in Lacan, is the loose change of the Thing. In his seminar on *Transference*, he emphasises the *agalma* in the transference as being something in the object that is a hidden element, defining it, but which has no form, no being, no nature, no status, no signifying structure. What else is he looking for in his subsequent *Seminars IX* and *X*? In the seminar on *Identification*, where he proceeds with the significantisation of Freudian identification, he extracts it from the imaginary, he emphasises the structure of the signifier. And in the seminar on *Anxiety* he contrasts this with the status, the worth, the true weight of *objet petit a* which he thereby frees up, and which he is going to seek out by superimposing "The Mirror Stage" onto "Inhibitions, Symptoms and Anxiety".[11]

This fourth paradigm frees up *objet petit a* as an element of jouissance, that is, it carries out an elementisation of the Thing. It makes the Thing into an element and into a multiple element. Because of this, the *objet petit a* is ambiguous from the start,

11 Lacan, J. "The Mirror Stage as Formative of the I Function as Revealed in Psychoanalytic Experience", *Écrits, op. cit.,* pp. 75-81, and S. Freud, "Inhibitions, Symptoms and Anxiety" (1926), SE Vol. XX, pp. 87-172.

for on the one hand it incarnates, it reproduces, the Thing, it is the elemental figure of the Thing, but, on the other hand, it is attached to the Other. It mediates in some way between the Thing and the Other. It is as if, in the *objet petit a*, the Other of the signifier imposes its structure on the Thing. It is, from new beginnings and on new bases, a renewed attempt at the significantisation of the second paradigm.

In a certain way, the *objet petit a* translates the significantisation of jouissance, while respecting, without doubt, the fact that it does not involve a signifier. Lacan abandons the notion of a signifier of jouissance. The very nature of jouissance seemed to him to be resistant to being pinned down by the term signifier. In place of the signifier of jouissance, which he marked with his symbol of capital phi – Φ – he gives us *objet petit a*. *Petit a* is without doubt an element of jouissance, as such substantial, which does not answer to the law of representing the subject for something else. It therefore has another structure, but one which is nevertheless endowed with a signifying property, namely that of presenting itself as an element. It is this elemental character of *objet petit a* which embodies its inscription in the symbolic order.

In *Seminar XI*, jouissance appears to respond to the signifying alienation of the subject in the form of the object, and it is this that Lacan calls separation. *Objet petit a*, this invention of Lacan's, has here the same elemental structure as the signifier and is at the same time substantial, whereas the signifier is material but without substance. There is signifying material, but there is a substance of jouissance, and it is this which makes the difference between the object and the signifier.

Paradigm 5: Discursive Jouissance

The elaboration of Lacan's four discourses corresponds to the paradigm that I call discursive jouissance. I find this paradigm in *Seminars XVI* and *XVII*, and in *Radiophonie*.[12]

What Lacan calls discourse is alienation and separation unified as one. This is the import of that phrase from *The Other Side of Psychoanalysis*, "There is a primitive relationship of knowledge to jouissance", which is to be understood as: "There is a primitive relationship of signifiers to jouissance."

Before this fifth paradigm, there was always in Lacan, in one way or another, a description of structure, of the articulation of signifiers, of the Other, of the dialectic of the subject, and then, in a second moment, the question was to know how

12 Lacan, J., *Seminar XVI*, unpublished, *Seminar XVII, The Other Side of Psychoanalysis*, 1969-1970, ed. J.-A., Miller, transl. R. Grigg, "Radiophonie", etc.

the living being, the organism, the libido were captured by the structure. What changes with the notion of discourse is the idea that the relationship signifier/jouissance is a primitive and primal relation. It is there that Lacan emphasises that repetition is repetition of jouissance.

"The signifier represents the subject for another signifier." This is a relationship which summarises symbolic alienation. But Lacan's discourses introduce, in some way, the notion that the signifier represents jouissance for another signifier. He does not employ this formula because it would create confusion with the former, or it would harden the logic. In representing jouissance, the signifier fails it in the same way that the signifier that represents the subject fails, since the empty set remains alongside it.

"The signifier represents jouissance for another signifier." This formula is derived from the one where Lacan summarises for the first time the relationship between subject and signifier, in the *Écrits*, page 694, in "The Subversion of the Subject": "Our definition of the signifier (there is no other) is: a signifier is that which represents the subject for another signifier."[13]

To start with, let us hang on to this formula which has the advantage of being explicitly by

13 Lacan, J., "The Subversion of the Subject and the Dialectic of Desire", *Écrits, op. cit.,* p. 693-4.

Lacan, and which is itself a formula derived from one made by the philosopher and logician Charles Sanders Peirce. Peirce's formula gave the definition of the sign in the following terms: "The sign represents something to someone." Lacan modified it, acknowledging his debt to it, under the form: "The signifier, unlike the sign, represents the subject for another signifier." This formula has the advantage of making the someone, the recipient, disappear and, on the contrary, of somehow making the authority of the system of signifiers attached to other signifiers appear in its place under the guise of the signifying Other.

It is enough to begin by examining the formal difference that there is between Peirce's definition and that of Lacan. Lacan's definition is clearly paradoxical when compared to Peirce's, in that the term being defined, the signifier, appears twice in the defining statement – "What is the signifier? It is that which represents for another signifier." This is formally circular. The point is to know what value one can recognise in this circularity of defining the signifier by the signifier via the subject, particularly when you compare it with the formally correct definition that Peirce gives to the sign. I have previously suggested the idea that Peirce's definition fits the sign in as much as the sign is *one*, that it appears in the form of a unity which is called on this occasion the symbol, outside a system, and which can have there an absolute value separated from the someone who deciphers it.

If Lacan introduces us to the signifier by a circular definition it is because it appears structurally and essentially as a binary, as evidenced in the definition itself. The signifier cannot be thought on its own. Or, to think it alone, to establish it alone, to place it alone, is an infraction of its normal logic. The binary that Lacan will use in his mathemes is the minimum articulation. It is an oriented binary, in the sense that it is one signifier having its value of subjective representation for another.

We have here the principle of a chain, of a repetition. In effect, if two is the minimum, the maximum is the countable infinity of signifiers. Under the two essential forms displayed by this binary, Lacan takes S_1 as a set of signifiers linked to the other signifier, itself unique. Playing on homophony, he came to call this *l'essaim* (the swarm). Or alternatively, by contrast with S_1 as unique, it is the other signifier that can be seen as having the multiplicity reunited in a set. This will be the case when Lacan distinguishes the *master*-signifier from the signifier *knowledge*, which is not unique but, on the contrary, set-like.

Lacan exploits these two versions of the initial binary. For example, on page 694 of the *Écrits*,

Lacan, as soon as he has posed it, moves from this first version, which I put here in the following form – *All signifiers represent the subject for another signifier that does not represent it.* This is a way to grasp the initial formula – *A signifier represents the subject for another signifier.* One can then, at this moment, consider the set of all signifiers that represent the subject, which can be distinguished from the other signifier which already finds itself in breach of the initial circular formulation. This version allows Lacan to introduce immediately a signifier that is an exception, that is, to give to this S_2 the value of $S(\cancel{A})$, that is to say, of a signifier that is supplementary with respect to the set of all signifiers that represent the subject, and at the same time inscribes itself as a minus in this set of signifiers that represent the subject.

To summarise. S_1–S_2 is the structure of language reduced to the signifier, a structure that is, for Lacan, present in the unconscious. This raises the following question: what sort of subject corresponds to this structure? This circular and paradoxical definition of the signifier implies a definition of the subject that conforms to it. The subject is that which is conveyed by one signifier for another signifier. Because no identificatory representation is complete, this representation tends to repeat itself.

Let us go so far as to say that if the subject is represented, it is to the extent that it is never presented, to the extent that it is never in the present. It is never anything but represented. This formula, which will be found written in Lacan's discourse under the form S_1 representing the $\mathcal{S}$, attempts at the same time to indicate that it is represented, yes, but that it always remains, in terms of structure, un-representable. Lacan never hesitated to couple the accomplished, which is there in the adjective 'represented' or 'articulated', with the impossible, which is there in the inarticulable and the un-representable. It is representing the un-representable that opens the signifier to its repetition, a repetition whose principle is the failure to completely achieve the representation that it aims at.

Lacan adds a second paradox, the one that the figure of alienation tries to harness. The subject, in itself quite un-representable, only emerges through the fact of being represented by a signifier. Lacan translates this by saying – *the signifier makes the subject emerge at the price of petrifying it.*

He tries to give us a sense of this by making us write S_1 in the set which includes it and where, invisibly, the empty set appears. This empty set is there as an element of the set, the one which can remain after the signifier is erased. In other words, when one writes S_1 as a set with only a single element, there is the representation of the subject, but, more secretly, there is the lacking being that is there behind it, and which would emerge if one erased the S_1.

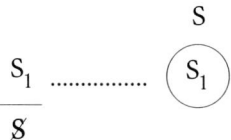

The set itself has no existence. It only begins to appear if a signifier is written there. This justifies Lacan in using this presentation to indicate that the signifier makes the subject emerge, and it makes it emerge at the same time that it fixes it in the representation that it has given it, thereby eluding its constitutive void.

From where does it make it emerge? Out of what primal material does the signifier make the subject emerge? This is a question which is hinted at but not developed by Lacan in his "Position of the Unconscious". The status of this primal material is a being – "A being", he says, "the being that does not yet possess speech." Before putting the apparatus of the signifier to work, we have the still mysterious instance of a prior being on which the apparatus inscribes itself, of a being from whom the signifier will fashion a barred subject.

This is what is highlighted by the operation of alienation on the side of the subject. Nothing of the signifier directly touches on what is in question in separation, since separation operates, according to Lacan, on a lack which is a loss of the body's life. To stay with this signifying mechanism, the signifier is the cause of the subject to the extent that one could say that without the signifier there would be no subject in the real, and that the subject is in the real always in the form of a discontinuity or a lack in ways that echo the empty set.

This subject is decomposed, declined in Lacan under forms of the truth that no description of the real will ever give – the truth inscribes itself, inserts itself in the discontinuities of the real. It is declined under the form of death, which is essentially how Lacan conceives of the impact of the signifier in the real, the impact, both somewhat pathetic and deadening, of the signifier on the real – mortification. It is also declined as desire. That is why it comes as no surprise when, on page 518 of the *Écrits*, in the "Agency of the Letter",[14] Lacan speaks of desire as dead desire, even though, according to Freud, it is precisely this signifying death that makes desire indestructible, quite unlike need. It is this signifying death that lodges desire in a cybernetic or electronic memory. This is why

14 Lacan, J., "The Instance of the Letter in the Unconscious", *Écrits, op. cit.*, p. 431. "... and which is the chain of a dead desire."

Lacan can say that the chain of repetition is that of a dead desire.

This is also why jouissance proper, jouissance as emotion, as affect of the body, cannot find a way to inscribe itself in this configuration. It is also why Lacan is led to state, in "The Subversion of the Subject", that jouissance lacks in the Other, that is to say, in order to exclude it initially from his signifying construction he is led to state that it cannot be spoken. He is then led to stress the antinomy between signifier and jouissance, and the antinomy between jouissance and the barred subject of the signifier.

What do we see in pages 694 to 698 in the *Écrits*?[15] These pages constitute Lacan's final attempt to try to formulate the status of jouissance in terms of signifier and signified. He says that jouissance lacks in the Other, but tries to apply the schema of the signifier and the signified to jouissance on the basis of the phallus. He invents a complex mechanism – on the basis of complexnumbers, in fact – which could articulate the signification of jouissance as forbidden – lacking, barred, mortified – with the signifier of jouissance, which itself cannot be annulled. He tries to account for this by distinguishing minus phi from capital phi, two signifying symbols of

15 Lacan, J., "The Subversion of the Subject and the Dialectic of Desire", *Écrits, op. cit.*

jouissance – minus phi (-ϕ) as signification and capital phi (Φ) as signifier.

But this is only the mark in his elaboration of the fact that the transcription of libido in terms of desire has not saturated the Freudian properties of the libido. For desire, even though agile, even this desire which slips in everywhere, imposing its quirks and varieties on everyone, is by definition a dead desire. Thus, despite the transcription of certain features of libido in terms of desire, there remains jouissance, which is what remains of the libido once it has been re-transcribed in terms of desire. This is impossible jouissance, beyond symbolisation, which he tries in "Subversion of the Subject" to take back into signification in the form of capital phi (Φ). When he speaks of *the signifier of jouissance*, he makes capital phi in some way the symbol of *das Ding*, a signifier rendered absolute. This is the culmination of his attempt to introduce jouissance into the signifying system.

This paradigm exploits in effect what has already appeared under Lacan's pen in "Subversion of the Subject", namely that at the same time that jouissance is forbidden, it can be said between the lines. This was already sketching the metonymy of jouissance, already suggesting that perhaps it is not only the barred subject, the lacking subject, which is carried by the signifier, but also jouissance as the lost object. In other words, this paradigm rests on an equivalence between subject and jouissance. That is why I have allowed myself to substitute the term 'jouissance' in Lacan's defining proposition for the term 'subject'.

We have here a determination of the nature of the being prior to the launching of the signifying system, and in a more precise form. The prior being is a being of jouissance, that is to say, a body affected by jouissance. This is why Lacan spells out fully in *Seminar XVII* [16] that the point of insertion of the signifying apparatus is jouissance. This point of insertion was never mentioned as such up until then and required a surreptitious substitution of the body for the subject, because before that we had a more or less autonomous and self-enclosed functioning of the symbolic order.

This is what leads Lacan, going beyond and against any idea of the autonomy of the symbolic, to propose that the signifier is the apparatus of jouissance. This renunciation, which is not achieved until paradigm 5, is in a way Lacan's abandoning of the autonomy of the symbolic. What had been approached up until this point as *'what is in motion in the signifying chain is the barred subject, truth, death and desire'*, is retranslated as *'what is in motion in the signifying chain is jouissance'*.

16 Lacan, J., *Seminar XVII, The Other Side of Psychoanalysis*, ed. J.-A. Miller, transl. R. Grigg.

What primitive relation is involved here? It is a double relation.

On one side, there is an annulment, a mortification of jouissance, but this time conceived of as a loss of jouissance, a fading of jouissance, of entropy, but situated as an effect of the signifier. This is no longer a loss considered as coming from the nature of sexuated life itself, as in paradigm 4, but a loss that is completely significantised. In other words, just as what Lacan had previously imputed to a fundamental prematurity, that is to say a natural lack, with the splitting giving rise to this duplication embodied in "The Mirror Stage", a gap which he subsequently significantised, so here what appears in paradigm 4 as a natural loss in life appears in paradigm 5 as an effect of the signifier. And Lacan changes the formulas around this signifying loss of jouissance.

The second aspect of this primitive relation, which responds here to the first, is a supplement of jouissance. Lacan then introduces the *objet petit a* as surplus jouissance, as a supplement to the loss of jouissance. As he says himself, it is a complete break with the terms of his paradigm 3. He says it on page 18 – *this is not linked to force or to transgression*. On page 19 – *there is no transgression. To slip through is not to transgress*. Or again, page 23, to exclude the term 'transgression' – *transgression is a lubricious word.*[17]

What is the term that he opposes to 'transgression'? It is signifying repetition pure and simple, which equals repetition of jouissance.

In *The Other Side of Psychoanalysis*, it is the signifying chain that Lacan presents as repetition or as knowledge. Signifying repetition had previously always been required by the subject for its signifying representation and by its division, which always leaves a part of the subject un-representable. All of *Seminar XVII* shows the repetition required by jouissance. As Lacan puts it: "Repetition is based on a return of jouissance. Repetition is directed at jouissance." This transposes what he had previously said about the subject, namely that jouissance is at once represented by the signifier whilst at the same time this representation is not exhaustive, but rather a failure, and it is precisely this that conditions repetition.

In this seminar, the emphasis is put both on the signifier as the mark of jouissance – he can say that "the master signifier commemorates an irruption of jouissance" – and at the same time he introduces the loss of jouissance which produces

17 "The relationship to jouissance is suddenly made to appear in a different light by this still virtual function called the function of desire. Moreover, this is why I'm describing what appears here as 'surplus jouissance' and not forcing anything or committing any transgression." *Ibid.*, p. 19. "We don't ever transgress. Sneaking around is not transgressing." And, "the lubricious word 'transgression'." p. 23.

the supplement of jouissance. By an analogy with the term 'entropy', which he borrowed from thermodynamics, he says – "Entropy takes over as surplus jouissance to be recovered." And elsewhere in the seminar – "Surplus jouissance takes shape as a loss."

From now on, access to jouissance is no longer essentially by way of transgression, but by way of entropy, the wastage produced by the signifier. Thus, Lacan can say of knowledge that it is a means to jouissance. There can be no better renunciation of the autonomy of the symbolic order. It is the means of jouissance in a double sense, in that it has the effect of a lack and that it produces the supplement, the surplus of jouissance. This also is what warrants his saying, in another formulation, page 76, that truth is the sister of jouissance. To say that it is the sister of jouissance is doubtless to say that it is inseparable from the effects of language and that it is especially linked to barred jouissance, jouissance as forbidden. This is to say that truth occupies the place where jouissance is annulled, mortified. We would have to add – *truth, the sister of forbidden jouissance*. This is why it is necessary to complete things with what Lacan has to say on page 202 – *truth is the dear little sister of impotence*.[18] Which

18 *Ibid.*, p. 174.

shows clearly that when he says *truth, sister of jouissance*, he aims at (-ϕ), what is, there, the effect of signifying annulment.

In other words, phallic jouissance, which is exemplary, perfect, paradigmatic jouissance, is forbidden, whilst something comes to make up for it, surplus jouissance, which is the embodiment of the loss of entropy. This repetition is conditioned and animated by the gap between (-ϕ) and *a*, that is to say, between the lack and its supplement. This is the principle of *encore*, of repetition as a fundamental form of the signifier.

This is the place to say that the signifier, the symbolic order, the big Other, this whole dimension is unthinkable without its connection to jouissance. This gives a new value to metonymy, since there where the subject was, there is from now on the lost jouissance. And this bears on the use and the demonstration that Lacan made previously when he gave a touch of formalism to the signifier. When Lacan gave us the scheme of *alpha*, *beta* and *gamma*, this was not at all thought in its connection with jouissance but, on the contrary, to teach us that there is an autonomous logic of the signifier independent of bodies, in some way transcending the body. Now there is indeed a return to the body. All that logic, whose elaboration still holds, is reinvested and motivated through the relation to the body.

In addition, this necessarily raises a new problematic about the end of analysis. The end of analysis, according to Lacan, always concerns the relationship of the subject to jouissance and the modification which it allows. But to think about this relation in terms of fantasy is not the same thing as thinking about it in terms of repetition.

There is a clear shift in Lacan between the relation to jouissance thought as fantasy and the relation to jouissance thought as repetition, since it is precisely thinking it as repetition which will lead him instead to giving a new value to the symptom. On this occasion I am using a capital R in a special sense to mean repetition.

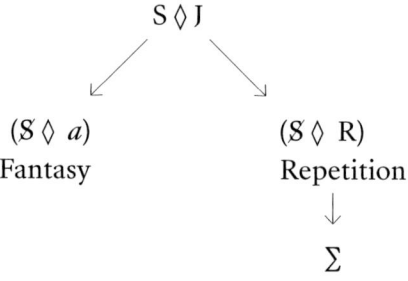

To think the relation to jouissance under the form of fantasy, is to think the obstacle under the form of a screen to be passed through. Indeed, I am led to say, in my own construction of these paradigms, that the crossing of the fantasy is in the end a variant of the paradigm of transgression. It is transgression dressed up in analysis as the end of analysis, with the invitation to go beyond, in the direction of the void, of subjective destitution, the fall of the subject supposed to know, and the assumption of the being of jouissance.

The anticipated effect nevertheless has both the form and the structure of an effect of truth, even if this effect of truth is the evaporation of the poor truth that is the sister of impotence. It is very different to think the relation to jouissance under the form of repetition. Repetition is to some extent the elaborated form of fantasy just as fantasy is like the concentrated form of repetition.

Repetition is what deserves to be called the symptom, which shows us in effect a repetition of jouissance and hence even a permanence but one that is not concentrated on the fundamental fantasy. It is rather a permanence which stretches out, which lasts. It is not as if it were condensed into the formula of the fantasy, which would have to be extricated, extracted, to permit a crossing.

The symptom, in the form that it takes in Lacan's final teaching, carries in itself the temporal development of this relation to jouissance, which does not lend itself to transgression, all the more so since Lacan calls it, in the seminar *The Other Side of Psychoanalysis,* the slipping-through, or what he sometimes calls the *savoiry faire*, the knowing-how, concerning the symptom. This knowing-how is a kind of slipping-through which precisely takes on a quite different value from an accomplished transgression. Evidently, this leaves a question about the end of analysis. Is it a question of putting an end to repetition, or is it rather a new use for repetition?

The idea of surplus jouissance – *plus de jouir* – clearly brings something new to jouissance. Jouissance as *das Ding* is thought of as a place beyond symbolisation and also as an identity. *Das Ding* is highlighted as a thing-in-itself, to distinguish it from the variations of the symbolic and the imaginary. When jouissance is presented as the *objet petit a* of the drive, it belongs in a list, on the basis of the list of drives drawn up by Freud, as developed by Lacan – the oral object, the anal object, the scopic object, the vocal object, and finally, to complicate things a little, the nothing. But when you think of jouissance as surplus jouissance, that is to say as that which fills in, but never exactly fills in, the loss of jouissance, that which, while giving enjoyment, maintains the lack of enjoyment, here the list of *objets petit a* increases and extends itself. The objects of sublimation are included in the list of *objets petits a*. The notion of surplus jouissance in Lacan has the function of extending the register of *objets petits a* beyond those objects in some way considered 'natural', extending them to all the objects of industry, culture, sublimation, that is to say, anything that can come to fill in for minus phi, without ever succeeding in completely doing so.

This is what Lacan calls the minor *objets petit a*, those that abound in society to cause our desire and mop up the lack of enjoyment, but only for a moment, as the repetition never stops. All that we are permitted to enjoy is in little bits. This is what Lacan calls, with an apt phrase, the crumbs of jouissance. We see our cultural world inhabited by substitutes for jouissance, which are little nothings. These are the crumbs of jouissance which give a particular style to our way of life and our way of enjoying.

To explain this, an increasingly clear division has to be introduced between the body and its jouissance, since in the end it is in the products of industry and culture that the body finds the wherewithal to feed its jouissance and its lack of jouissance. This even implies introducing, as Lacan does in *The Other Side of Psychoanalysis*, a cut between libido and nature. One needs to add that it is precisely this cut between libido and nature which introduces a connection between libido and culture.

When Lacan writes in his discourses the signifying couple, the barred subject and the *objet petit a* in the fourth position, and when he rotates these terms, it is clear that the *objet petit a* admits to functioning as a signifier. Jouissance itself is as close as possible to being reduced to the functioning of a signifier, clearly with the reservation that it is not a signifier. The couple 'alienation and separation' become almost a relation of cause and effect. In the first place, the signifier is the cause of jouissance, the means of jouissance, which implies that jouissance is the aim of the signifier. And, secondly, the signifier rises up from jouissance, emerges from it, since it commemorates it.

This fifth paradigm is completely conditioned by relationship. The relationship between signifier and jouissance, between knowledge and jouissance, is primal, but this relation is even closer for being primitive. Lacan insists on denying anything that might stay outside the relation between signifier and jouissance. He shows on the contrary to what degree the introduction itself of the signifier depends on jouissance, that jouissance is unthinkable without the signifier, and that there is a sort of primitive circularity between the signifier and jouissance.

Paradigm 6: The Non-Rapport

With paradigm 6, which I take from the seminar *Encore*,[19] an inversion takes place with respect to Lacan's entire trajectory up to this point, while

19 Lacan, J., *Seminar XX, Encore*, On Feminine Sexuality, The Limits of Love and Knowledge, 1972-1973, ed. J.-A. Miller, transl. B. Fink, London/New York, Norton, 1998.

pushing the indications of paradigm 5 to their conclusion. What distinguishes this sixth paradigm is that it starts out from the fact of jouissance. It is in a way a return to the Thing, to the extreme of the attempt to reduce the Thing to that *objet petit a.*

At the culmination of this paradigm, I have placed the formula that can be found in the last chapter of *Encore*, which is the following: "The signifier is the sign of the subject." This formula constitutes a kind of return to Peirce. Lacan's movement leads him in some way to define the signifier as a sign, with the attendant difficulty of integrating this latest expression into his conceptual framework. It is with the aim of reaching the threshold of this formula, which appears to contradict the definition which Lacan himself said was the only definition of the signifier, that I go back to the wish, which was also Lacan's wish, for a canonical formula for the signifier.

In *Encore*, Lacan begins with the fact of jouissance, although his starting point was the fact of language and the fact of speech as communication addressed to the Other. In relation to language and speech, to the structure which supports it, it was a question of the capture of the living organism. In the fifth paradigm, with the notion of 'discursivity', Lacan went as far as posing a primal relationship between the signifier and jouissance. I myself have been trying to transcribe this in terms of representation: the signifier represents jouissance.

In paradigm 5 Lacan truly cuts the branch on which all his teaching was sitting, and in the final part of his teaching there will be an attempt to build another conceptual apparatus out of the debris of the preceding one. In *Encore*, he puts into question the very concept of language, which he considers to be derivative, not primary, in relation to what he calls *lalangue*, which is speech before its grammatical and lexicographic ordering. Similarly, he puts into question the concept of speech, now conceived of not as communication but as jouissance. Whilst jouissance was, in his teaching, always secondary with respect to the signifier, and even though in paradigm 5 he develops it into a primal relationship, language and structure, hitherto treated as primordial givens, will now appear, in this sixth paradigm, as secondary and derivative.

What he calls *lalangue* is speech disconnected from the structure of language, which now appears as derivative with respect to that primary exercise and separated from communication. It is under these conditions that he can then pose a primal inclusion of jouissance, speech and *lalangue* under the heading of the jouissance of blahblah. In this paradigm, the concept of language, the earlier concept of speech as communication, as well as the concepts of the big Other, the Name of the Father, and the phallic symbol are all pushed to the point of collapse into semblants. All these terms find themselves reduced to a function of stapling together elements that are fundamentally disconnected.

This paradigm is based essentially on the non-rapport, on disjunction – the disjunction of signifier and signified, the disjunction of jouissance and the big Other, the disjunction of man and woman under the heading of *There is no sexual rapport*. This is truly the seminar of non-rapports. All the terms that, in Lacan, provide connection – the Other, the Name of the Father, the phallus – which used to appear as primordial terms, even as transcendental terms since they condition all experience, are reduced to being connectors. In place of transcendental terms of structure, coming from an autonomous dimension, prior to experience and conditioning it, we have the primacy of practice. Where there was transcendental structure, we have a pragmatic, and even a social pragmatic.

I represent this last paradigm, which is indexed on disjunction, by these two Eulerian circles whose intersection is marked as empty.

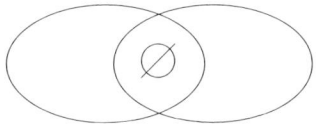

This empty intersection can be filled in by several terms which we can consider, from this perspective, as substitutes, operators of connection between the two sets. These 'intersectors' are various and belong, in Lacan, to two large registers. Whatever can fill in for this missing connection comes under either 'routine' – a deprecatory term to qualify what is glorified under the name of tradition, the heritage of past ages – or else can be written into the register of 'invention', or indeed, if we are optimistic about what unfolds in front of our eyes, the experimentation of the bond. The current debate, concerning the sexual bond in particular, plays out, as foreseen by Lacan thirty years ago now, between 'routine' and 'invention'.

Lacan's sixth paradigm allows us to locate the place where routine and invention are operative. In giving you this schema, I thematise as such the concept of non-rapport that Lacan puts to work with regard to the sexual, making us repeat: *There is no sexual rapport.* The surprise on reading his seminar *Encore*, when one was acquainted with Lacan, when one got into the spirit of his teaching, comes with the evident extension of this concept of non-rapport, which needs to be set against that of structure. The reference to structure led us to establish, to take as given, a multitude of relations which we simply called articulation. This word 'articulation', which we exemplify by the structural minimum S_1-S_2, is the formulation of relations, in the plural, to which, without further thought, we attribute the quality of being real in the form of necessity, that is to say, that which never stops writing itself.

The seminar *Encore* introduces another kind of relation that limits the empire of structure. This other type of relation needs to be generalised. It is the non-rapport which shakes up everything that we were mistakenly inclined to consider as given under the banner of structure: the articulation S_1-S_2 in so far as it has signifying effects, the Other as prescribing the conditions of all experience, and also the paternal metaphor, the nodal articulation of the Freudian Oedipus, which is part of the structural order, that is to say, of a relation that is taken as given, a given relation that, of necessity, never ceases to be written.

Structuralism, in the end, was nothing other than the sanctification, under the guise of science, of a certain number of relations that are precisely called into doubt by the following question: would it not rather be a case of non-rapport, that is to say, a relation made up of routine or invention? The empire of the non-rapport, in Lacan's final teaching, goes on to question the pertinence of trying to operate on jouissance on the basis of speech and meaning. This indication is like the summit of what the empire of the non-rapport is capable of, and, in this respect, the invention of the psychoanalytic discourse as well.

Concerning psychoanalysis, Lacan was very careful to distinguish between what it was capable of at the time of its invention by Freud, in its earliest days, and what is possible for it when this very invention becomes routine. Halfway through the century of psychoanalysis, he was already pointing out that the effects of this invention were questionable, becoming blocked by its routine use. He gave psychoanalysis a new lease of life for a further fifty years by his own invention. We must not hide from ourselves that today Lacan's re-invention is itself progressively blocked by its routine use, and is it not for us once again to fix it by re-inventing it?

This reinvention is what we are invited to by this sixth paradigm, that based on the non-rapport. The starting point for this perspective is not 'there is no sexual rapport' but on the contrary a 'there is' – there is jouissance. Lacan's original starting point in 1952 was in fact 'there is psychoanalysis.' It exists, it functions. That is to say, at the point we are at, that there is a satisfaction which comes from the act of speaking to someone, under the conditions of psychoanalysis, and from the various mutative effects that follow. Someone is spoken for –

psychoanalysis makes this clear – and, in speaking for someone, there follow the effects of truth which reorganise the subject from top to bottom. The relation to the Other appears there at the origin, at the beginning, as a given.

The point Lacan now arrives at is: 'psychoanalysis does not work.' And he asks himself why it does not work. It is quite another thing to start from the evidence that 'there is jouissance'. There is jouissance as the property of a living body. This is a definition which brings back jouissance exclusively to a living body. All there is for psychoanalysis is a living body – one that speaks, of course. Moreover, the 'and which speaks' [*et qui parle*] is again, for Lacan, in this seminar, something that must be described as a mystery – he ends one of his lessons of that year with this. Put another way, the assumption is, 'through the body' [*par le corps*]. You find this on page 26 – *Isn't that precisely what psychoanalytic experience presupposes? – the substance of the body, on the condition that it is defined only as that which enjoys itself.*[20]

This starting point implies a disjunction between jouissance and the Other. This point of departure which privileges jouissance is by itself enough to establish the non-rapport between jouissance and Other. Here 'disjunction' means

20 Lacan, J., *Encore, ibid.*, p. 23.

'non-rapport'. This makes the Other of the Other appear in the form of the One. Around this time, Lacan had come to stress the One as the true Other of the Other. In thinking about the Other of the Other, one sees the Other and then the Other of the Other, in some way as above and guaranteeing the former.

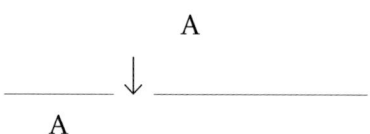

We then pose the question – Is there truly a guarantee? And the answer is no, there is no guarantee. Here, the Other of the Other appears as below, not above, in the form of the One

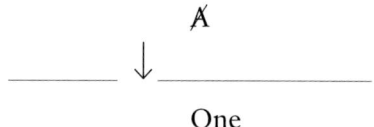

Starting from jouissance leads back to a One-all-alone, separated from the Other. Here it is the Other that appears as the Other of the One.

This very elementary schema is useful for grasping what it is that Lacan is concerned with throughout this seminar, namely, to emphasise everything in jouissance that is jouissance One, in other words, jouissance without the Other. One can even hear the title of *Encore* as a homophone, as Lacan suggests at one point – *En-corps*. It is the body that is at stake here, far more than the repetition he spoke of in his *The Other Side of Psychoanalysis* in the marriage of jouissance and knowledge.

This is to rediscover, in psychoanalysis itself, what prevails today in the social bond, that which we call, without further thought, modern individualism, which indeed renders problematic everything that is relationship and community, including even the marital bond, where even those whom we can call conservatives, those who sanctify routine as tradition, are irresistibly taken by the movement of invention, to establish through the means of positive law – as voted for in parliaments – relationships between individual atoms. The starting point found in jouissance is the true basis of what appears as the extension, as the madness even, of contemporary individualism.

Lacan's seminar is thus a declension of jouissance One. Just as, originally, he tried to show that jouissance was from top to bottom, from head to toe, imaginary, now he shows that jouissance is fundamentally One, which is to say that it does without the Other.

The primary requirement is to situate the place of jouissance without any idealism. At this point, the place of jouissance, as the cynics perceived, is the body itself. What Lacan shows is that all effective jouissance, all material jouissance, is jouissance One, that is to say jouissance of the body itself. It is always the body that enjoys itself, by whatever means available.

Another figure of jouissance One that Lacan exposes is the jouissance that is especially concentrated on the phallic part of the body. There is clearly a possible dialectic between the jouissance of the body itself and phallic, that is to say, specialised jouissance, but if Lacan puts the emphasis on phallic jouissance, it is to the extent that it is another type of jouissance One, of the One-jouissance. He describes this phallic jouissance as the jouissance of the idiot, of the solitary, a jouissance which is set up in the non-rapport to the Other. That is why Lacan pins this figure of jouissance One as masturbatory jouissance.

A third figure of One-jouissance is jouissance of speech. Throughout Lacan's teaching we have been led to believe that speech connects to the Other as addressed speech, communicative speech. However, the jouissance of speech only appears here in Lacan as a variant of jouissance One, that is to say cut off from the Other, which indicates that speech is essentially jouissance and not communication with the Other.

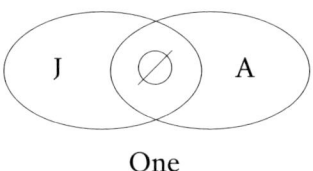

One

This is what is at stake in blahblah, as he puts it, which is the last degree of the pejorative qualification of speech. Blahblah, means precisely that it is not a question of communication, that from the perspective of jouissance speech does not aim at recognition, or comprehension, but that it is only a modality of jouissance One. There is a body that speaks. There is a body that enjoys in different ways. The place of jouissance is always the same, the body, which can enjoy through masturbation, or just by speaking. Although it speaks, this body is not thereby linked to the Other. What matters to it is its own jouissance, its jouissance One. This is seen in psychoanalysis, particularly in shorter sessions. It is not the complex elaboration of signification and the solving of an enigma that keeps it going. It is through taking speech as a specific mode of satisfaction of the speaking body.

Fourthly, Lacan goes as far as to implicate sublimation at this point, and to give us a version of sublimation that does not involve the Other. This is the last straw, because what was essential in Freud's elaboration of sublimation, when he invented the term, when he grasped its import, was that sublimation was essentially, inevitably, recognition by the Other. For sure, Lacan makes use of the connection between sublimation and recognition by the Other. Sublimation only finds completion through the satisfaction of the Other. But, in *Encore*, Lacan gives us a version of sublimation as not involving the Other, but as being the legitimate outcome of the speech of jouissance, solitary speech. You find on page 109 – "When one leaves it all alone, the speaking body always sublimates with all its might."[21] This is really to indicate to us that it is in the place of the jouissance One that sublimation finds its true home.

Thus, jouissance One, this One-jouissance presents itself as jouissance of one's own body. It does not follow on from bodily jouissance. It is both interpolated and displaced. Sometimes, Lacan is interested in the connections between the different jouissances. He contrasts them, defines them in relation to one another. Jouissance One, examined closely, might appear as bodily jouissance, as phallic jouissance, as jouissance of speech, or as sublimatory jouissance. In each case, it is not, as such, related to the Other. Jouissance as such is jouissance One. This is the reign of the One-jouissance.

All this construction renders the jouissance of the Other extremely problematic. Its very

21 *Ibid.*, p. 121.

existence is cast in doubt. In any case, if it exists, it is not on the same level as jouissance One. Jouissance One is real, whilst the jouissance of the Other now appears as a problematic construction.

From the perspective of jouissance, the jouissance of the Other is sexual jouissance, the jouissance of an Other body differently sexed. When starting from the signifier, from communication, where wit rules, it is the Other subject that answers you. It is the place of code, the place of the signifier, that which ratifies. But, starting from jouissance, the Other is the Other sex. To begin with, jouissance One, solitary, is fundamentally asexual, so much so that until then, for Lacan, the relation to the Other was primal, structural. Structure denatures the world, but at the same time, more subtly, structure can naturalise, that is to say, structure itself appears to be beyond question, a priori. But from the perspective of jouissance, the relation to the Other will appear, on the contrary, as problematical and derivative.

It is on this basis that "*There is no sexual rapport*" is justified, becomes in some way inevitable. "*There is no sexual rapport*" means that jouissance as such comes under the sway of the One, that it is jouissance One, whilst sexual jouissance, the jouissance of the body of the Other sex, has the distinction of being specified by an impasse, by a disjunction and by a non-rapport. This is what allows Lacan to say that jouissance has nothing to do with a sexual relationship. Jouissance as such is One, it falls under the One, and it does not, of itself, set up a relation to the Other. "*There is no sexual rapport*" means that jouissance is basically idiotic and solitary.

This concept of non-rapport which dominates the sixth paradigm puts a limit to the concept of structure. When, for example, Lacan tried to find a formula for the Oedipus complex under the form of metaphor, as in the mathemes, he emphasised the fact that structure is something that is written, which never stops writing itself, and which then appears as a necessity which imposes itself on everything that shows itself, on all phenomena. In this way, structure is seen, in structuralism, as a kind of *a priori* form, as incorporating given categories, already present and unfalsifiable, which cannot be done away with. Structure was always seen as omnipotent when exposed. However, its limitation appears here in the sexual jouissance of the Other as sexed being, because here there is a relation given up to contingency, to the chance encounter, a relation subtracted from any necessity.

With *Encore* Lacan began to explore everything that was freed from necessity, everything that is, on the contrary, given up to routine and invention. In other words, it substitutes the pragmatic for the transcendental of structure. 'Transcendental' means exactly what conditions experience, the markers that delimit all possible experience – with a Kantian stress which is there in Lacan in "On a Question Preliminary to any Possible Treatment of Psychosis". We are much more demanding as to what is necessary and what is not. Structure is full of holes and, in these holes, there is room for invention, for novelty, for connections that have not always been there.

It is rather like a version of the Enlightenment. The eighteenth century was fascinated by – and catalogued – all the ways in which other peoples handled sex, how they articulated jouissance and the Other by other means. Since when, as a rebound from this freedom glimpsed for a moment, the nineteenth and twentieth centuries have to some extent erected a so-called globalising routine, have deified what remained of tradition, and have sought to give it shape.

We, however, live with the reopening of this empty intersection. With gathering momentum, the transcendental gives way to the pragmatic. This does not mean that there is no structure, that everything is semblance. There is the real, but it is much more difficult today than formerly to isolate and discern what is structure and what is real.

Translated by Janet Haney
Revised by Roger Litten

Milanese
Intuitions

Jacques-Alain Miller

Milanese Intuitions
Jacques-Alain Miller

PART ONE

We were reminded about politics, in the inter-
val since my previous class, by an irruption that
came as a surprise. I must admit that my taste for
surprises goes to the point that I welcomed this
one with a smile. For a moment. I then realised to
what degree the calculations of the experts, like
those of the multitude, can be proved false and
thwarted. How evidence nurtured for many years
could collapse and produce a mass effect, which
has certain traits of depression or panic, but also
of defence and mania. We have witnessed a kind
of social manic defence. A political mobilisation

These two lessons (15 and 22 May 2002) form part of Jacques-Alain
Miller's 2001-02 course, The Disenchantment of Psychoanalysis:
The Lacanian Orientation, an annual seminar delivered within the
framework of the Department of Psychoanalysis, University of Paris
VIII. The first of these lessons was delivered three days after Miller
had been in Milan delivering an improvised lecture for a study day
marking the event of the foundation of the Lacanian School of the
Freudian Field in Italy. That lecture was given on the theme of the
study day: "Psychoanalysis in the City". A version of these lectures, translated by Thelma Sowley, was published in Mental No. 11, 2002, pp. 9-16, and
Mental No. 12, 2003, pp. 5-14. It is published here in a revised translation.

followed, which has not spared psychoanalysts and certain of their associations, which is why I am referring to it here.

Prior to this we had been far from suspecting what was going on in the depths. We were laboriously studying the concept of counter-transference and the history of the psychoanalytic movement over the past half-century. This led me to welcome the opportunity given to me last Sunday, on the occasion of the effective creation of the School of the Freudian Field in Italy, to speak in Milan on the theme of "Psychoanalysis in the City". I am going to share with you my Milanese intuitions about the relationships between the unconscious and politics and try to develop them here.

The Unconscious and Politics

In Milan I took as my starting point an assertion by Lacan that can be found in his 1966-7 seminar, *The Logic of the Fantasy*. I came across this phrase just before my departure in a book that has just been published here in France which presents a kind of psychopathology of political life. This is the quote from Lacan: "I do not even say 'politics is the unconscious' but simply 'the unconscious is politics.'"

The person who quoted these words simply rejected the second formula, "the unconscious is politics," as abrupt and absurd. He accepted the first formula, "politics is the unconscious", but with reservations. At least he has the merit of grasping that these two formulas are not equivalent. It is not: if A = B, B = A. Yes, he says, there is something of the psychic in politics, but politics is not only the unconscious, even if there is in it something of the unconscious, or fantasies, dreams, lapses, anxieties...

What is the point of quoting Lacan if it is only to blunt the edge of his argument, to extract something so impoverished from it? It's certainly not even a definition of politics, because fantasies, dreams, lapses and anxieties are not only part of politics. They are everywhere that there is "man", in quotation marks, whether in contemplation or in action, in different ways of saying and doing things, in all cultures, in the state or in society, in solitude or in the crowd.

Nothing remains of Lacan when you make this kind of commentary on his phrase, whereas there is in Lacan's formulation a flash that at least provokes a moment of surprise before disappearing into the night where all cats are grey. There is something in Lacan's saying that is worth hearing, and this is precisely what has been amputated without adding anything in the commentary to which I have referred.

The *agalma* of this saying is the formula "the unconscious is politics". One can at least remark that it is a formula that is within the competence of a psychoanalyst, while the other formula, "politics is the unconscious", proposes a definition of politics, which is more risky when pronounced by a psychoanalyst, because defining politics is not his business. This is precisely why Lacan says "I do not even say 'politics is the unconscious', but simply 'the unconscious is politics'".

This is how I took up the theme that our Italian colleagues proposed to deal with, namely "Psychoanalysts in the City". Are psychoanalysts in the city? This is up for discussion. But in any case, if Lacan's formula is true, psychoanalysis is in politics. This is what allowed me to find a thread to develop the theme under discussion.

The reflections I presented in Milan were improvised. Since Sunday, I have advanced a little on the question, but I will lead you along via the way I followed. It must be said that what I presented was translated simultaneously into Italian by someone standing alongside me. This obviously limited my movements. This is why I introduced things – as I'll do here – as a succession of numbered propositions or reflections.

First Reflection: Politics Is the Unconscious.

Lacan says: "I do not even say 'politics is the unconscious'". He thus situates his assertion in the register of denegation, if you will, saying what he has to say while saying that he does not say. From the logical point of view, while recoiling from transforming this statement into a thesis, Lacan stresses that if it were a thesis, it would take us further than the other.

Is this, nevertheless, the thesis of nobody, a thesis without a father? It seems to me that if this thesis had a father, it would be Freud. This thesis "politics is the unconscious" would be a reading of Freud, because Freud says something like this, that politics, at least at the time when he was writing, is reduced to the unconscious. This is the thesis that can be extracted from his *Massenpsychologie*, where he analyses collective formations as formations of the unconscious having the same identificatory signifier and of the same cause of desire.

It seems to me that this thesis is evoked in Lacan's assertion insofar as Freud considers politics from the angle in which it is reduced to the unconscious. The important word here is that of reduction, reduction of politics to the unconscious. That is why this thesis, even though derived from Freud, lends itself to objections which are all of the same type: namely, that there is more to politics than what falls under the unconscious. As soon as one finds oneself faced with a reductionist thesis, the objections are variations on the theme: 'that is only partial, things are more complex than that'. I mentioned *Massenpsychologie* but one could read *Civilisation and its Discontents*, and *Moses and Monotheism*, in the light of the same thesis.

One could reject this thesis by saying that in the end Freud is not talking about politics but rather the unconscious, taking his examples from the field of politics. Let us remark that in any case this field is dominated, structured, by the instance of the father, that Freud approaches it within the paternal regime. This is why the terms that organise his approach to this theme are those of identification, censorship, and repression, including the repression of jouissance.

Second Reflection: The Unconscious Is Politics

This thesis, qualified as abrupt, as absurd, and which the author allows himself to dismiss with the wave of a hand – I left for Milan irritated by this dismissive attitude to a formula that is more modest than the previous one, since it proposes a definition of the unconscious. This is how it is in Lacan and it is much more reasonable. We know so little about what the unconscious is, it is so unrepresentable, that it is implausible and very risky to define anything on the basis of the unconscious. On the contrary, it is always the unconscious that is to be defined, because we do not know what it is. The unconscious is never for Lacan the *definiens*, the term that defines, it is always the *definiendum*, that which is to be defined.

Take, for example, the formula "the unconscious is structured like a language". This is a thesis that assumes that we already have the definition of language. In fact, Lacan uses the one that Saussure and Jakobson produced. Of course, in the formula that I am commenting on today there is no "like". One must therefore ask oneself how to define politics in such a way that it makes sense to say that the unconscious is politics.

What amused me was that, after coming across the comment that irritated me, I opened a second recent book, by a political scientist who has probably read Lacan, Marcel Gauchet,[1] who just published a collection of articles under the title *La démocratie contre elle-même* with articles that span twenty years. In this book I came across a definition of politics that, I must say, fitted like a ring on the finger. "Politics consists specifically in this: it is the place of a fracture in the truth."

This is a beautiful definition, one that is at the same time undoubtedly infiltrated by Lacanianism and even perhaps a certain Merleau-Pontyism. The term 'fracture' is one that this author likes. We find in this collection the famous formula of "the social fracture", which must be in one of his articles of the years 1990-91, and which was taken up, in 1996, by a young demographer and came to

---

1 Gauchet, M., *La démocratie contre elle-même*, Paris, Gallimard, 2002.

the attention of a figure in French politics. But initially, indeed, it is this Lacanoid political scientist who found this notion of fracture.

He defines politics as a field structured by S of big A barred, S(Ⱥ). This defines a field where the subject painfully experiences the fact that truth is not one, that truth does not exist, that truth is divided. This is a definition of politics that retains all its virulence in the times in which we live, a moment that is still, after all, a "post-totalitarian" moment, into which we entered in 1989 with the fall of the Berlin Wall – an event that not everyone applauded, let me remind you.

I do not necessarily validate this category of totalitarianism, which was used for political propaganda during the twentieth century. It is a convenient approximation. Totalitarianism was a great hope, it enchanted the masses of the twentieth century. In the twenty-first century, it is something that we barely recall. Totalitarianism was the hope of reabsorbing the division of truth, of establishing the reign of the One in the field of politics in accordance with the model of *Massenpsychologie*. At the level of its aspirations to concord, to harmony and reconciliation, totalitarianism is impeccable, terms that must resonate with all the echoes they have in the discourse of President Schreber.

The triumph of democracy, which has the wind in its sails in the spirit of the times, at least for a good part of the globe – obviously things are different in China, where we hear about the emergence of a new pathology, death from overwork, in a region where the word "union" would really be a new idea – does not generate the same enthusiasm. It even seems to have a depressive effect, in that it would imply consenting to the division of truth, a division that takes the objective form of political parties engaged in an intrinsically insoluble contradiction given that the truth is condemned to be divided.

Gauchet puts it nicely, with a lyricism worthy of Merleau-Ponty: "From now on, we know that we are destined to encounter the other under the sign of an opposition without violence, but also without return or remedy. I find myself faced not with an enemy who wants my death but with a contradictor. There is something metaphysically terrifying in this pacified encounter."

I like the link made here between terror and pacification. It seems that we are in a process without end. "A war can be won," says Gauchet, "while this confrontation never ends." Hence the paradoxical idea that the pacification of the public space goes hand in hand with a private, intimate, subjective suffering, and that at the same time that we celebrate the virtues of pluralism, tolerance and relativism, we also experience a truth, I quote, "which is only offered in the form of a rupture." Not bad!

We would have to consider whether we have here only a surface effect and that more deeply politics remains a question of you or me. We'll come back to this some other time.

The definition of the unconscious by way of politics is something that goes to the roots of Lacan's teaching. "The unconscious is politics" is a development of Lacan's initial definition that "the unconscious is the discourse of the Other." This link to the Other intrinsic to the unconscious is what animates the teaching of Lacan from the outset. This remains the case even when we specify that the Other is divided and does not exist as One.

"The unconscious is politics" is a formula that radicalises the consequences of what Freud discovers in his analysis of the *Witz*, namely that the witticism is a social process that is completed in the Other, in the one who recognises the *Witz* as such. This is the notion of the formation of the unconscious as a social process that finds satisfaction in the recognition of the Other. The happiness that the *Witz* brings is precisely due to the reception that it receives in a community reunited in a moment of laughter.

Third Reflection: The Unconscious Is Political.

The Freudian analysis of the *Witz* justifies Lacan in articulating the subject of the unconscious to the big Other and qualifying the unconscious as trans-individual. It is this analysis which is the basis of the intuition of Lacan's teaching on this theme. We can pass from "the unconscious is trans-individual" to "the unconscious is political" from the moment when it appears that this Other is divided, that it does not exist as One.

For this reason "the unconscious is political" does not say the same thing as "politics is the unconscious". "Politics is the unconscious" is a reduction, a formula that brings politics back to the structure of the unconscious. You will remember that when Lacan formalises what he calls the discourse of the master, he says at the same time that it is the discourse of the unconscious. He thus gives us the key to many of Freud's texts.

"The unconscious is politics" is the opposite of a reduction. It is an amplification, an extension, it transports the unconscious out of the solipsistic sphere, to introduce it into what is called the City, to make it depend on "History", on the discord of "universal discourse"– in quotation marks since it is discordant– at each moment of the series that develops from it.

Fourth Reflection: The City Does Not Exist

Let's go back a bit to our starting point. Psychoanalysis in the City! The term is questionable because the City no longer exists. Today the City is imaginary. When we say the City, it is understood as a metaphor for politics, but in *Wirklichkeit*, in current historical times, politics no longer develops in the form of the City. The City is a nostalgia, an afterglow, which is also imaginary in the sense that people look for it today on the television.

In Milan, I quoted the editorial from the previous day's *La Republica*, which was devoted to a criticism of the Prime Minister of Italy, Mr. Berlusconi, who personally owns three of the six Italian television channels and directs the other three as President of the Council. In this article, television was qualified as *agora*, the modern *agora*, highlighting the degree to which our modern *agora* is crippled. The first move of the ancient *agora* would have been to ostracise Mr. Berlusconi, obeying the principle that a citizen who is too powerful must be sent into exile for ten years, just to teach him how to live.

At the same time this journalist considered television as the place where a consensus is elaborated and diffused. This highlights the fact that the *agora* in the era of the market has nothing to do with the *agora* of ancient times, which was a space of social homogeneity that presupposed the exclusion of those who were denied democratic privilege.

When we evoke the City today, it is simply as an imaginary place of the political order as social homogeneity. But not only does the homogeneous City no longer exist, but the Nation State itself is shaken, it is in question, is turns out to be porous, waning to the extent that some go so far as to prophesy its disappearance. Others, on the contrary, try to revitalise it, but even beyond the City, it is now the Nation State that is in question. Rather than talking about psychoanalysts in the City, we should thus consider the question of psychoanalysts under "globalisation", an approximate concept, but one that is certainly more operative than that of the City.

We are very far removed from the homogeneous space of the City. What is called globalisation is a glimpse of a social space where nothing is still in its place, something that we touched on in speaking of the opposition between the ancient and new worlds. But here it is the very notion of place itself that is subtracted, accompanied by what we amiably call losing our bearings. When nothing is left in its place, the category of lack itself tends to become obsolete. Lacan explained the notion of symbolic lack with the example of the well-ordered library where a book is missing from its place. What we call globalisation is precisely this space where the category of lack itself tends to become obsolete.

Fifth Reflection: Freud and Queen Victoria

Here we need a new reflection that I'm going to call Freud and Queen Victoria, recycling one of Lacan's jokes from his seminar. He had been reading Lytton Strachey's book about Queen Victoria, and he got a laugh out of his audience by saying that without Queen Victoria there would have been no Freud, that Queen Victoria was the historical cause of Freud. This joke, which deserves to be taken seriously, sketches the link between the birth of psychoanalysis and the disciplinary society, with a reaction against a society that involved such strong prohibitions, censoring any expression of sexuality, a notion that must of course be modulated given that transgressive forms have always existed, but precisely as transgressive: that is to say that the prohibitions remained in place.

On the contrary, it suffices to think of the banalisation of the sexual spectacle today, from the pornographic film to Catherine Millet's latest book, to understand that we have entered another regime of sexuality. It's no longer a question of Queen Victoria but of Queen Catherine!

This is not the first time that I have emphasised that the whole of Freud's conceptual apparatus remains marked by the disciplinary era: prohibition, censorship, repression. It is even this that allowed the junction between psychoanalysis and Marxism, whether in the form of Freudo-Marxism or that of 1968-style protest.

It must be noted that the Lacanian renaissance of psychoanalysis in the 1960s and 1970s is contemporary with the era described by Antonio Negri, who spends every night in prison on account of having been the inspiration for the Red Brigades. In his book *Empire*[2], Negri tries to give a doctrine of the international far left. He notes, on page 272-3 of the English edition: "In the period of crisis, throughout the 1960s and 1970s, the expansion of welfare and the universalisation of discipline in both the dominant and the subordinate countries created a new margin of freedom for the labouring multitude. In other words, workers made use of the disciplinary era [...] in order to expand the social powers of labour..."

Negri emphasises that the very concept of liberation owed something to the disciplinary forms of domination. What he tries to think through in this book is what comes after this disciplinary society. What he calls "*impero*", empire, is a regime that no longer proceeds by discipline, that is to say, by prohibition and repression, which makes transgression problematic, along with the very idea of revolution and liberation.

2 Negri, A., and M. Hardt, *Empire*, Cambridge, Massachusetts/London, Harvard University Press, 2000.

Obviously we can recognise the filiation of Negri's inspiration. Negri is the descendant of Deleuze and Guattari.[3] He recycles *Anti-Oedipus* which is now thirty years old. But let us not forget that *Anti-Oedipus* is itself a reading of Lacan. Lacan thought psychoanalysis during the disciplinary era, but he also anticipated psychoanalysis in the imperial era. This is what we tried to bring up to date with "the Other that does not exist".

Sixth Reflection: "Lacan and Queen Jouissance"

It might be said that Lacan's historical role has been to bring Freud up to date, preparing psychoanalysis in the era of globalisation for the new order that Negri and Hardt call *Impero*. If we approach things from this angle, we can distinguish three moments, three phases in which Lacan's historical role has been fulfilled.

The first phase is that of the formalisation of psychoanalysis in the disciplinary era. First, by the formalisation of the concept of the unconscious on the basis of the algorithm of the sign; by the unifying formalisation of the Oedipus complex, castration, and repression through the concepts of the Name of the Father and metaphor; and by the formalisation of the libido through the

3 Deleuze, J., and F. Guattari, A*nti-Oedipus, Capitalism and Schizophrenia*, London, The Athlone Press, 1984.

concepts of desire and metonymy. The classic Lacan is Freud formalised.

We then have a second phase, which we can perhaps today classify as a transitional phase, where Lacan carries out a subversion of Freud via a subversion of the function of the Name of the Father, which is pluralised but also displaced when he attributes the operation of repression not to paternal prohibition but to the fact of language as such. Again there is a subversion of the concept of desire linked to prohibition, a concept that is displaced by that of jouissance; rather than lack, he emphasises what fills the lack. This is how he defines the function of the *objet petit a,* which of course remains attached to the theme of lack – this is why I say that this phase is one of transition – but where what prevails is what comes to fill this lack.

And, in the third phase of Lacan's work, what we call his last teaching, the essential term is that of jouissance, which has no opposite. Until then jouissance had been in tension with the repressive and mortifying signifier. Well, in the third phase of Lacan's reflection, the signifier itself becomes an operator of jouissance. Jouissance had also been in tension with pleasure, but precisely in the third phase of Lacan's teaching, the opposition between pleasure and jouissance tends to dissolve. It is not that all validity is subtracted from it, but pleasure becomes a certain regime of jouissance.

The level of the drive, which unlike desire is not intrinsically articulated to a defence, is the level that Lacan located with the proposition that "the subject is always happy", always happy at the level of the drive. The concept of the drive is the concept of a function that is always satisfied. The only question is that of its mode of satisfaction. Is it satisfied directly or indirectly, painfully or pleasantly, etc? Axiomatically, the drive is always satisfied.

This corresponds to the exit from the disciplinary era, which was organised around prohibition and transgression. Everything now becomes a question of arrangement. We no longer dream of an outside. There are only trajectories, arrangements, and regimes of jouissance. This is what Lacan tried to translate in terms of the Borromean knot. The Borromean knot is already an effort to find a way out of a binary of structural oppositions, and the disciplinary organisation that this division implies.

I would like to come back to this notion of the disciplinary society. It comes from Michel Foucault and was highlighted by Deleuze in terms of the opposition between the disciplinary society and the society of control, indicating two regimes of mastery. The disciplinary society is the era in which there is a relation of exteriority between the apparatuses of repression and of training, on the one hand, and the subjugated on the other. In this era the prominence of domination and indoctrination allows for frontal opposition to oppression. Here one can identify the oppression and the figures of the oppressors. Resistance can thus take support from the forms of coercion. Foucault thus considered the institutions of the prison, the factory, the asylum, the hospital, the school, the university, institutions which presuppose a clear differentiation between in and out.

This becomes of interest when we distinguish what was already being modified thirty years ago, namely, that domination had ceased to be obviously exterior and was now somehow immanent to the social field. The well-known mechanisms of domination that the Marxists could analyse were being internalised and being diffused in a more subtle or invisible way by the communication or information society. If one could still speak of domination, it was no longer typified by eminent, repressive, isolated figures. Rather a form of control that is no longer external circulates above all through flexible, modular, fluctuating networks – to the point that Negri uses the formula of "autonomous alienation" to designate a form of mastery that is no longer external but internal, to which the term extimacy might be more appropriate.

I have a little more to say, but I do not think I'll get to the end this time, any more than I did in Milan. I must reassure you right away that Negri's book is not the new *Das Kapital*. It is rather like a great poem. It is by someone who has studied Spinoza, who is Spinozist – he describes with pathos a world that is somehow without operators, an empire that is no longer the imperialism of anyone, a globalisation which is everywhere and nowhere, which flows, which multiplies, and at the same time has no borders and no exterior. It's very repetitive. It's more like a chant, it's like the *Divine Comedy* of globalisation, something that I do not take quite seriously, except as the work of a poet, that is, very seriously.

Seventh Reflection: The Analytic Treatment in the Era of Globalisation

The treatment is undoubtedly marked by the three phases that I have distinguished. Conceived initially as a treatment that was distinct from a medical treatment, it was ordered in relation to an ideal of maturity and a norm of personality. Lacan even went as far as speaking of the achievement of the personality and the effective realisation of the Oedipus complex and of castration. And even when he speaks of phallic disidentification, this still supposes that there is an ideal and a norm in operation. As long as Lacan was in this phase of his teaching, even while disputing the ideal and refusing the norm, the question was pressing precisely because the treatment nevertheless remained besieged by, occupied by, the insistence of the norm and the ideal.

We could distinguish a second phase, marked by the demedicalisation of the treatment. I am not making a precise chronological distinction, but this is the moment when analysis could be conceived as an experience and no longer as a treatment. The word 'experience' is important. It means it is the place where something happens for you. We could compare this with the current doctrine regarding the building [*édification*] of stores, as you see in New York, in Los Angeles, in Beverley Hills, where new stores have to respond to what is called *experientialisation* – that is to say, the transformation of shopping into a unique and irreplaceable experience. Otherwise everyone would just do their shopping on the Internet.

In a way, Lacan "experientialised" the analytic treatment before anyone else, putting the emphasis on the activity of the patient, the analysand, and the production of a new subject. This crystallised in his notion of the pass, with the end of analysis thought in the mode of a transgression. The crossing of the fantasy is a passage beyond a limit. This is why I put it in what I called the transition phase. The third phase, which is specific to the regime of globalisation, appears at the end of *Autres écrits*, where the pass, as a procedure, is resituated as a successful narrative that satisfies an audience.

Moreover, it is well known that in the Freudian Field the products of the pass, the Analysts of the School, have been taken up in a process of spectacularisation. Indeed, the Analysts of the School have been invited to speak before the largest audiences that could be assembled on an international scale. We have been criticised for this. Those who criticised us for it are those who would like to return to the disciplinary era, but precisely because of our openness, our sensitivity to the times, we have indeed ourselves been captured by the spectacularisation of the procedure of the pass.

And here, if we follow the scattered indications of Lacan, which do not invalidate the previous constructions – everything is compatible, it's like in Italy, on one level you have the pagan temple, then you have Mithras, and in the end you have the Church, all in the same place. Freud also uses this example when speaking about the unconscious, so we should not think that we are forgetting the previous moment if we follow the indications of Lacan – the end of the analysis, in this third phase, is stripped of the pathos of the beyond, of transcendence, of crossing. On the contrary, the emphasis is more modestly on the changes in the regime of jouissance that can be achieved in the treatment. But it is stripped of the absolute – it is truncated. It is above all a question of the end of analysis at the level of the drive. And drive satisfaction has no opposite. And so the reference here is not to a crossing but to the passage from one operating regime to another.

The famous formula "there is no sexual rapport" is inscribed within this framework. This formula signals the definitive erasure of the norm that secretly ruled psychoanalysis, which was precisely the norm of the sexual rapport. The exit from what kept psychoanalysis in the disciplinary era is achieved through the formula: "there is no sexual rapport". And we must complete this formula: "there is nothing but jouissance".

This is what happens in the era of globalisation, where we have already been for some time. This level renders inaudible the themes of maturation and achievement and opens up the space of invention – of sexual invention, of creativity without norms. This is obviously congruent with the inclusion of jouissance in human rights, in law as such; it is congruent with the juridification of jouissance. And this goes hand in hand with the promotion of the symptom, under the new name given to it by Lacan, the *sinthome*, with a new writing to indicate that it is a symptom that has no opposite.

What Lacan calls *sinthome* is the symptom when there is no longer any opposite, when the subject is, as such, condemned to this symptom, or, to avoid this theological and disciplinary vocabulary of condemnation, it must be said that the symptom appears as the regime proper to jouissance, that jouissance is necessarily experienced as a symptom by the subject, or rather by the living being who speaks.

There are still a number of reflections to come. The eighth concerns what this epoch involves in terms of the depreciation of psychoanalysis.

Eighth Reflection: The Depreciation of Psychoanalysis

It must still be said that the operators of psychoanalysis are today experiencing their act under the threat of depreciation, in the same way that psychoanalysis – whether IPA, Jungian, Lacanian, or neo-Lacanian – is besieged by psychotherapy. This is really the little end of the telescope. What I am calling the depreciation of psychoanalysis is an indication of how psychoanalysis is going to be classified in the future. If one refers to a particularly astute American economist on this point, he ranks psychoanalysts and psychologists in the great category of *attention givers**, those who give attention. This is a very valuable commodity in the state of mass anonymity and the pressure of the mass media. We are looking for someone who pays attention to us – psychologists, psychoanalysts, babysitters, butlers, private gym instructors, etc. He constructs this category and shows that it is one of the two growing categories in the economy. But this growth obviously goes hand in hand with a certain deskilling. This accomplishes a certain depreciation of the position of the analyst.

PART TWO

We shall devote this meeting to the political unconscious, which the movement of history has led us to stumble upon, interrupting the laborious study that we had undertaken on counter-transference. I will pursue my reflections, those I shared with you last time. The formula "the unconscious is political" that I extracted last time produced quite a splash [*pavé dans la mer*] – that is to say, it made waves both in practice and in theory, although "theory" is here perhaps too big a word around which I should put quotation marks.

Reality Staged by the Structure

Theory, when we try to produce it – theory in the present – is nothing more, at least in psychoanalysis, than a sinuous trail, a trail we blaze in an attempt to catch up with what has already taken place and which advances by itself. Theory and practice in psychoanalysis are not symmetrical or parallel. It is important to note that in psychoanalysis there is a lagging of the theory that is not contingent, not accidental, but which is undoubtedly structural, at least as far as its elaboration is concerned. And this elaboration is of course in tension with the very knowledge that it is supposed to elaborate. It would be beautiful if this knowledge expressed reality being accomplished according to a necessary order, in accordance with Proposition 7 of Book II of Spinoza's *Ethics: Ordo et conexio idearum* – the order and connection of ideas – *idem est* – are, is the same as, since *ordo et conexio* are united there – *ac ordo et conexio rerum* – the same as the order and the connection of things.

This is an essential proposition, the very ideal that animates Lacan's structuralism, on the condition that the order and connection of ideas in this formula be replaced by the order and connection of signifiers. This is what Lacan designated as the pure and simple combinatory of the signifier. This combinatory was supposed to define relations of necessity, the same as those encountered in reality. This is the conception of knowledge against which we measure our efforts, given that it is the conception of a knowledge that is not a representation of reality, but which aims to be identical to the very principle of the effective development of reality, identical to the principle of its production, its *Wirklichkeit*.

In this conception, structure is neither an ordered description of reality nor a theoretical model elaborated at a distance from experience. See here Lacan's critique of Lagache in the *Écrits*, page 544[4], which constitutes a classical reference for us. Lacan claims to overcome the difference, the opposition, the contradiction that he calls the antinomy of these two conceptions of structure, as description and as model, by introducing a third mode of structure according to which structure is produced in reality itself and determines effects therein. For Lacan, these effects are effects of truth, effects of jouissance, effects of subject – the truth is itself an effect, as is jouissance and also the subject.

It is in this direction that we must understand Lacan's proposition that can be found on this page, according to which the structure operates within experience as – I have already quoted this formula which is especially valid, at the time Lacan used it, for the fantasy – the structure operates within experience "as the original machine that puts the subject on the stage". Let's explain these terms.

---

4 Lacan, J., *Écrits, The First Complete Edition in English*, transl. Fink, B. New York/London, Norton, 2006, p. 544.

'Machine' is a word which designates a signifying articulation, combinatory and determinist, whose variations are strictly conditioned. Some years later, Lacan will give an example that serves as a reference in his cycle of the four discourses. The staging of the subject supposes, in fact, that the combinatory machine is behind the scenes – that it does not give itself to be seen, that it is hidden – which makes us believe that it is at a distance. Being hidden means that it escapes any descriptive phenomenology, that it is not enough to let it be, to let be what is there, in order to access it. The expression "staging of the subject" has an ambiguity that reflects the actual division of the subject. That is to say that the subject is staged, he is an actor, he is not the director and at the same time he is a spectator – reality, for him, is staged by the structure.

What is added to this articulation by qualifying this machine as original? Without doubt, Lacan means that it is not derived from anything anterior in the strictly genetic sense, which he criticises on this page, but in the combinatorial sense. And original also means unique. This machine is proper to each subject, it has to be reconstituted in the analytical experience for each subject. But it would be unreasonable to limit the validity or the inspiration of this proposition to analytic experience in the strict sense of the term, because the subject is not the individual. Lacan also speaks about the subject of science, for example, and one can very well consider that the discontent analysed by Freud concerns the subject of civilisation.

This is what we are confronted with when we are put on the alert, as we have been recently. We realise that we are confronted with the original machine that stages the subject of civilisation at the present time, and that this also conditions the analytic experience. Here we have the outline of an ambition constantly resumed, redrafted, to recompose this original machine from what is given to us of its effects.

The Unconscious Is of the Order of the Social Bond

I need to clarify a point which I mentioned last time when I quoted Lacan's formulation from a quotation that had been made of it: "I do not even say 'politics, it's the unconscious', but simply 'the unconscious is politics'." I indicated that this formulation was taken from *The Logic of the Fantasy*, quoting it without having referred to the stenography, which I have since done. I would therefore like to add here, before continuing, some considerations on this point. First, because we find in the stenography the formula "unconsciousness is politics". But I am in favour of correcting this stenography to read "the unconscious is politics".

The passage that was quoted, which I took up, is part of a sentence that I would like to relate to you more completely. This is what Lacan said: "If Freud has written somewhere that anatomy is destiny, there may come a moment, when we have come back to a healthy perception of what Freud discovered for us, when we will say, I do not even say, etc."

This complement shows that the matrix of Lacan's statement is indeed a formula of Freud's, and that Lacan opposes what Freud said in echo of the Emperor Napoleon to what Freud discovered for us, that is to say, to what Freud really said. What Freud really said is not what Freud said. It is in fact the inspiration of all of Lacan's teaching that is concentrated there. What Freud really said is not that anatomy is destiny. What Freud refers to in an attempt to explain the subjective difference of sexuation is not the anatomical body. Moreover, anatomy does not even determine hysteria, since, as Lacan notes in *Television*, hysterical conversion does not obey anatomical partition.

Here one could bring into question the living body alongside the anatomical body, in order to distinguish them from each other. Of the living body, in so far as it speaks and speech conditions its jouissance, one could perhaps say that it determines destiny. But in this passage of his Seminar, Lacan operates a displacement from "anatomy is destiny" to "the unconscious, is politics". And he explains this by saying: "What bonds men to each other, what opposes them, must be motivated in the logic that we are trying to articulate" – which at that time was the logic of fantasy.

"The unconscious is politics" is related to what bonds and opposes "men", in quotation marks, to one another, that is to say the unconscious is of the order of the social bond. It is this conception that, a few years later in the teaching of Lacan, will be put into matheme by the cycle of discourses. The unconscious is of the order of the social bond – let's introduce this gloss – precisely because there is no sexual relation. We could go so far as to say that where there is sexual relation, where the sexual bond is programmed, well then, there is no society.

Of course, we were enchanted to dream about the society of bees, or that of ants. Maeterlinck, when he was not making us dream of Pelleas and Melisande, enchanted us during our childhood by describing to us these societies which provided a utopia, precisely because they were, because they are – what they were and what they are is exactly the same thing – societies without politics. It is societies without politics that furnished us with utopias. One could say that theocracies have tried to achieve a society without politics or that ethnological structuralism presented us societies equipped with elementary structures of kinship, which for that reason are apolitical, something that was subsequently challenged.

Today, it does not seem abusive to propose that there is no society without politics, and that, correlatively, the unconscious is political. This is what Lacan was elaborating during those years. After having shown that the unconscious is produced in the relation of the subject to the Other, he went on to show that it is produced in relation to the Other sex, precisely along this path coming up against the absence of the sexual rapport and the interposition of the *objet petit a*.

"Being Rejected" and the Political Demand of the Other

This statement by Lacan – to be a little more complete – is situated in his seminar in the course of a reflection on the formula "being rejected", "being refused", on the basis of considerations on masochism that he takes from Bergler's work *The Basic Neurosis*.[5] Bergler introduces this status of the subject, "being refused", about the oral stage and he locates the "being refused" – to be refused which would be the principle of the behaviour, the attitude of certain subjects – he bases this "being refused" on a "being refused by the mother". This

5 Bergler, E., *The Basic Neurosis. Oral Regression and Psychic Masochism*, New York/San Fransisco/London, Grune & Stratton, 1949.

would be the masochistic desire that the subject would create, at the level of the oral drive, which would allow him to bemoan this injustice and take enjoyment in it. "Being refused", which would be the reason for the subject's complaint, would find its motive in the desire to save himself from engulfment by the maternal partner.

In the very movement of producing the formula that "the unconscious is politics", Lacan makes a fundamental objection to Bergler which situates Lacan's political position quite well, the position that he promoted and animated in his teaching, namely: but why should one be accepted rather than rejected? Why should one have to do what it takes to be accepted? Who says that this table where one would have to want to be admitted would always be benevolent? What is behind this is the metaphor of the *Symposium* and those who are not admitted to the banquet.

This clearly situates the position of subversion that was Lacan's, which, it must be recognised, remains topical today. At the time, current affairs were concerned with what was taking place in what Lacan calls a certain small region of South-East Asia, the Vietnam War. Lacan commented on what was at stake in the following way – which resonates and can still resonate today when Asia has probably gradually been regularised, but another zone of the planet, not yet! – "It is a question of convincing them that they are wrong in not wanting to be admitted to the benefits of capitalism." At that time we discovered that they preferred to be rejected from it. It is in this respect that Lacan invites us to reflect on certain significations – especially on the signification of "being rejected" – and it is in the wake of this that he introduces, without developing it, his "the unconscious is politics".

What Lacan adds – despite its brevity it is still capable of evoking some echoes for us – is that one is only rejected if one offers oneself. This leads him to recall as key to the neurotic position the close relationship of the subject to the demand of the Other. With respect to this demand, he says, we must suppose that there is for the neurotic "a necessity and perhaps a benefit in being rejected." Later, Lacan would perhaps have spoken of the jouissance of being rejected.

This involves a very precise clinical indication, which is that one must think twice before trying to force a subject not to be rejected, because being admitted to the banquet of the others might not be the best thing that can happen to him. Lacan says that having the prejudice that it is better to be admitted to what you consider to be the benefits, to index the analytical operation on this, can give the analyst a persecutory function. This would be to give to what the analyst considers to be the principle of reality the value of a forcing, rather than to consider as valid in itself the desire to be rejected, that is to say, the desire not to submit to the demand of the Other.

This is also indicative for the present moment of civilisation where it is not the desire of the Other that is so present but rather the insistence of its demand, of its political demand in the form of democracy and the market considered as values to which your welfare is linked. In such a way that what is in fact a preference becomes incomprehensible, even monstrous, preferring to be rejected from the order of these benefits. This in any case indicates a position of reserve for the analyst with regard to these master signifiers of the specifically political demand of the Other.

This is what I wanted to add, to modulate what I said last time about Lacan's formulation, relying on the quotation I had taken from an author.

The Depreciation of Psychoanalysis

I had arrived at my eighth reflection on the depreciation of psychoanalysis. I announced the resource that I was able to find *The Future of Success*,[6] a book by political economist Robert Reich, who is part of the lineage of essayists who emphasised social narcissism in the era of

6 Reich, R., *The Future of Success*, New York, Knopf, 2001.

globalisation, the first of whom, in the 1980s, was Christopher Lasch, author of *The Culture of Narcissism.*[7]

His idea is that mass anonymity enters into contradiction with the desire for celebrity induced by the mass media object, hence the big question of how to attract attention. The answer to that question is present in what we know of the motivations of the recent killer in Nanterre. He found in his act the opportunity to realise Warhol's "to be famous for fifteen minutes", managing to get his name on television and in the newspapers at least once.

Robert Reich's idea is that there is an economy of attention: a demand for attention and an offer of attention, therefore a market for artificial attention. It is within this register that he inscribes psychoanalysis, including what he tells us about its growing diffusion in the United States, because from his position he does not need to differentiate between psychoanalysis, psychotherapy, or any other form of "psy".

He therefore delineates the development of a whole sector of specialised activities in the service of attention. This allows him to create a category where we also find personal gym teachers (*personal trainers**), those who do the shopping for you because you do not have the time (*personal*

7 Lasch, C., *The Culture of Narcissism: American Life in an Age of Diminished Expectation*, New York, Norton, 1979.

shoppers*) and the entire set of psychological spiritual advisers. He thus isolates the sector of attention givers, among whom he also inscribes domestic staff, *baby-sitters**, etc.

It is as an economist that he creates this category, and he indicates that it is one of the two sectors that are growing the fastest in today's society, the other being the sector of creative workers. He prophesies that in the future – at least in the United States, but for him the United States predicts the future of less developed societies – if you do not have what it takes to be a creative worker, you will probably find yourself working more and more in the sector of specialised attention givers. He says: "Your children, if they are not creators, innovators, will find themselves in this sector, which is promising, but at the same time is destined to deskilling. Essentially, if the economy is growing within essentially two sectors, the creators and the attention givers, the *attention givers**, are those who do not manage to get into the other sector. It is also growing, but in the direction of increasing deskilling [*déqualification*]. We can nevertheless be reassured that he puts psychoanalysts and psychologists among highly skilled workers, but he still lists them in the same category as butlers and *babysitters**.

This analysis is not ill-intentioned, it is not primarily aimed at psychoanalysis. It is a study of the new working conditions in the context of the new economy. It was moreover followed a few months later by the bursting of the bubble of the new economy. But it is all the more valuable for not being polemical. It gives the impression of a depreciation of psychoanalysis by the fact that it is not apprehended in terms of a desire for truth but in terms of a demand for personal attention.

It is a depreciation, but at the same time we know that something has changed in the classical dynamics of the analytic treatment. It is this modification that is conceptualised, in his own way, by Robert Reich. Admittedly, this is not the ultimate truth of psychoanalysis, but it is useful to relativise the attention we pay to the fine internal differentiations that fragment the analytic environment but disappear under the eye of the economist. We see where the analytic act is ranked. It is striking that in this classification, the activity of the psychoanalyst, psychotherapist or psychologist appears to be closer to *babysitting** than to medicine. There is still, in the end, an effect of truth that arises there despite the reservations that we might have regarding this classification.

The Machine of the Not-all
We must continue to look at ourselves in such a way that we are exotic for ourselves. This is

probably social phenomenology, but it is from these elements that we have to try to reconstitute the original machine of today's civilisation.

The father. We can see everything that still links psychoanalysis to the myth of the father, and we can see that society, with all the modifications of the era of globalisation, has ceased to live under the reign of the father. Why not say it in our own language? The structure of the all has given way to that of the not-all. The structure of the not-all implies precisely that there be nothing to serve as a barrier, nothing in the position of the forbidden. Prohibition appears as contradictory to the movement of the not-all. The structure of the not-all is what is described on the social and political level by Antonio Negri as *impero*, as the empire that develops precisely without encountering limits. This is what for us corresponds to the structure of the not-all, transposed to the level of what we can no longer call social organisation.

We should not be surprised to find here the not-all, since Lacan introduced this not-all in his text *L'Étourdit*[8], where he responds precisely to Deleuze and Guattari's *Anti-Oedipus* – as shown by the end of this text – reconceptualising what these authors had tried to grasp. The function of the father is in effect related to the structure

8 Lacan, J., "L'Ètourdit", *Autres écrits*, Paris, Seuil, 2001, pp. 449-496.

that Lacan found in masculine sexuation. This is a structure that comprises an all with a supplementary and antinomic element that constitutes a limit, which allows the all to be constituted as such, allowing organisation and stability. This structure is the very matrix of the hierarchical relationship.

The not-all is not a whole that contains a lack. On the contrary, it is a series in development without limit and without totalisation. This is why the term 'globalisation' vacillates for us because the question is precisely that there is no longer any all, any whole, and that in the current process what constitutes an all and what constitutes a limit is under threat, vacillates. What is called globalisation is a process of de-totalisation that puts all 'totalitarian' structures, in quotation marks, to the test. It is a process in which no element is provided with an attribute that would be assured to it in principle and forever. We do not have the security of the attribute, but its attributes, its properties, its acquired assets are precarious. The not-all entails precariousness for the element.

We see every day, in fact, what had been the respect for tradition giving way to the attraction of the new. This phenomenon, abundantly described, is staged for us by the machine of the not-all. To take an example that is revealing, at least for those who are aware of it, the Catholic Church in the United States is undergoing a veritable martyrdom. We have seen a cardinal – you know what a cardinal is, a prince of the Church – summoned to come to court and answer questions, the kind of questions in American trials that you may have an idea of through the detective novels of Erle Stanley Gardner or Perry Mason novels. The questions asked are short, factual questions that follow one another. You have to answer exactly what is asked of you by yes, or no, and then the other leads you by the nose. Well, the well-named Cardinal Law, of Boston, was subjected to such a questioning a fortnight ago. I found on the Internet a transcription of the whole of this interrogation, absolutely disconcerting for those who have some attachment to tradition. And the gall to demand transparency from the Catholic Church! And the renewed mistrust, including on the part of American Catholics, with respect to the role played by a potentate living in a microscopic state in Italy. This is truly a sign of the times. One sees age-old practices surrounded by a universal respect today becoming strictly undecipherable, rejected by the spirit of the times.

One truly has the feeling that there is an original machine that is staging completely unprecedented scenarios like that of Cardinal Law humbly answering the questions of the prosecutor, namely: name, first name, explain to us what a cardinal is, explain to us what a diocese is, and so on. We're not there yet in old Europe, but we can see what promises to be irresistible in this original machine.

By a certain short-circuit, if we admit that the machine that stages what we call globalisation is the not-all, that is to say – for Lacan, who relates it to feminine sexuation – that we can refer to this structure what we observe of the rise in society of values said to be feminine, the values of compassion, the promotion of the attitude of listening, the politics of proximity, which must now affect political leaders.

The spectacle of the world perhaps becomes decipherable, more decipherable if we relate it to the machine of the not-all. Of course, the practice of listening is only proposed as political on the basis of the absence of response. Listening itself becomes a response to the silence of the master. This is the political use of intersubjective communication, namely, that you will never receive any message other than the one you yourself have sent.

This also makes us weep for the traditional element, which was already grasped half a century ago, namely that the virile is under attack, and we observe, at least in developed societies, a certain popularity problem for the warmongers. This is, of course, correlative to a call to authority, to a return to order, a desperate appeal to the reign of the master signifier, itself in the process of being eradicated. In any case, we observe the tension between the functioning of the machine of the not-all that exacerbates nostalgia for the master signifier and this appeal to the master signifier, all the more exacerbated as it appears detached from the rest, and all the more insistent in that it clearly appears as supplementary.

In the social not-all, on the contrary, the signifier no longer comes to us in organised blocks. The signifier tends to present itself to us in discontinuous fragments, for example in the form of immediate information, which is why the Americans are studying *information overload**. What we call information is the way the signifier comes to us, no longer organised but discontinuous, essentially fragmentary, and with an effort to try to add to it an organisation that is always in the process of being undone. Even Robert Reich can spot this as a pathology of disorientation.

The Pluralised S_1 and the Subject Without Bearings

This is why sociologists have isolated, in the face of the overdose of information, the subjective strategies that consist in retreating into limited zones of certitude. Descriptively, it is quite powerful. This was already announced by the promotion of the postmodern, by Lyotard who generalised the concept of the postmodern. He had already characterised it in the past as the de-structuring of the great filters of knowledge, that is to say the traditions, the consecrated authorities, what he called the meta-narratives, the stereotypes. These are all organisations of the signifier, various forms of the discourse of the master, which had the merit of operating a simplification and formalisation of reality, of disseminating models of coherence, models of coherent behaviour under the authority of authorised bodies recognised as such.

One might hope that, in this era of de-structuring of the filters of knowledge, by some miracle schools would be capable of operating this simplification and formalisation of reality, even though all the apparatuses that supported them have been cracked, attacked, besieged, or are at least in decline. What the sociologists have discerned is that globalisation is accompanied by individuation. What is impaired is the mode of living together, the social bond, which exists in the form of uprooted and dispersed subjects, and which induces for each both a social duty and a subjective demand for invention.

It is the very telling formula of *living my own life**, to live my own life precisely in its difference from the others, that highlights the decadence, the decline of the collective organisation of models. This leaves the subject confronted by a demand – which he takes as his own – for the invention and valorisation of his individual style of life. This is the epoch we had called that of the Other that does not exist, and of what Bourdieu tried to recompose as the mechanisms of distinction, which already belongs to another epoch. Today the mechanisms of distinction that he evokes are scrambled – he presents to us a simplified world, almost the world of his childhood.

It is here that we see in Lacan's teaching how he both isolated and at the same time questioned what he called the S_1, the central signifier of identification. He isolated the master signifier in his matheme of the discourse of the master, which has as its central agent the master signifier, which is pre-postmodern. It is the discourse of the pre-postmodern master:

$$\frac{S_1}{\$} \rightarrow \frac{S_2}{a}$$

So the first movement isolates this central signifier. But as soon as he had isolated it, he pluralised it, multiplying it, getting us to hear the value of *essaim*[9] in the expression S_1, in order to say that there is not just one. There are several, and on the contrary, nothing assures that they are

9 [TN: *Essaim*, or swarm, rhymes in French with S_1.]

anything but chaotic, even if the swarm moves together. A constellation of signifiers rather than the unicity of the master signifier.

And then, alongside this matheme of the discourse of the master, he sketched the matheme of the capitalist discourse, a modification of the discourse of the master, where the barred subject is put in the place of this S_1.

$$\frac{\$}{S_1}$$

This is not so much a promotion of hysteria as a promotion of the subject without bearings. It is in function of this original machine that one can observe, as the sociologists do, the constitution of limited zones of certitude which, on a small scale, give these bearings.

The Bubbles of Certainty

We can of course explain that the structure of the not-all is abstract and that, in fact, in reality, this is not the way it happens, because in effect the machine of the not-all involves the ever more insistent constitution of micro-totalities whose multiplication, and the investment of the subjects that are taken into it, translate the presence of this machine. These micro-totalities offer niches in the not-all, shelters, a certain degree of systematicity,

stability, codification, and thus permit the resti-
tution of mastery but at the price of an extreme
specialisation. It is necessary to choose a very
restricted field of signifiers, a very limited field of
knowledge in which mastery can be restored.

There is an example that I found that seems
to me very indicative, in a study that was published two years ago, which concerns a phenomenon that has been observed in Japan called "the
otaku effect". This is in an article I know only
second-hand, which is quite difficult to find, and
is called "The Otaku Answer to Pressing Problems
of the Media Society".[10]

That's what was isolated in Japan. These are
always categories that can be considered suspect but
are nonetheless indicative. It's about the behaviour
of adolescents, or grown-up adolescents – we do
not know where it stops any more – who become
fanatics of a very small zone of new technologies.
They become complete specialists in what appears
to be a very futile phenomenon of the media society
or of certain types of manga, or of an idol, as they
say – actor, model, etc – or a technology generally
linked more or less to the computer or video games,
or they accumulate a knowledge as complete as
possible about that by keeping up with the latest
rage. Outside of this, the complete disinterest they

10 Grassmuck, V., *Man, Nation & Machine: The Otaku Answer to
Pressing Problems of the Media Society*. Available online.

show in their contemporaries is remarkable, to the extent that it can be said that in Japan they no longer look people in the face. "An *otaku* prefers to stay alone to pursue his hobby peacefully. He is obsessively devoted to one area of interest. The objects of his passion usually belong to pop culture." There are also military objects – it's Japan. "The essence," says the sociologist in question, a certain Grassmuck, "the essence of the *otaku* lifestyle has nothing to do with a specific argument, but is related to how to relate to a theme." The category that seems to be in use in Japan is not built with reference to the theme of interest, but to the way of relating to this theme. "The *otaku* has a monomaniac personality. His strategy is to collect information reserved for a single section of human knowledge and to discard everything else. The *otaku* is looking for a small zone of knowledge about which he wants to know everything." And so it is generalised to all the behaviours induced by the information society, the media society, which consists in wanting to know completely at each moment what is *in** and what is *out**.

This has also spread in France in magazines, to tell you the *in** and *out** so that you know from one moment to the next how you can be located in the crowd.

I cannot judge the relevance of this description for Japan, and we can even consider that it is not necessarily well constructed for the present state of civilisation in France, but there is still something in psychoanalysis which lends itself to be conceptualised as an *otaku* response.

There is something of the *otaku* lifestyle in the analytic associations, in the Societies, in the Schools of psychoanalysis. One could even say that the analytic experience itself is of the order of the *otaku* response – the analytic experience as a search for certainty, and also because the relation in itself, which is established in the analytic framework, restores a zone of certainty to the subject. Analysis puts uncertainty to work, but it is within the framework of an at least hypothetical certainty, hence the extreme value of the framework that we observe in the IPA, and an extreme valorisation of the framework, at the same time indefinable.

Moreover, with Lacan, one can perhaps observe the same thing in the definition of the analytic discourse which is presented by Lacan himself as a transformation, therefore a version[11] of the discourse of the master, that is to say like a bubble of certainty to which the subject is all the more attached as they are immersed in the social structure of the not-all.

---

11 [TN: *version* here, as well as the usual sense, has a sense of "turning around" in which can be heard a sense of the turning of the movement from one discourse to another.]

It must certainly be added that if psychoanalysis is a bubble of certainty, at the same time it radiates in society since it is put to work in advertising, and has taught politics the manipulation of truth. It really taught politicians that truth is an effect, which gave birth to *spin doctors**, truth doctors, truth-manipulation experts. We have also recently observed in France the extraordinary promotion of a marketing specialist, who became prime minister – it is a first – and apparently chosen because of that. At the same time, we have already mentioned the way in which the theme of listening, which is drowning psychoanalysis on one side, is spreading, but it must also be recognised that it comes from it.

Psychoanalysis in the Era of Globalisation

Let us try to look rapidly at how the changes in our clinic are related to the era of globalisation and how they would be animated by the machine of the not-all.

The classical clinic, the one that we have been formed in, has as its pivot the Name of the Father and is distributed according to the positions of the subject with respect to the Name of the Father. It is here that we distinguish different modalities of desire – desire that is unsatisfied, impossible, anticipated, etc. – as well as different modes of defence. Our classical clinic responded essentially to the structure of masculine sexuation, the structure of the all and the antinomic element. This is what allowed us to have these tight, rigid, powerful classifications that founded the notion of Lacanianism for generations.

Well, let's say that the contemporary clinic, the one that we have been dealing with for some years now, inclines to the other side, to the side of the not-all. This clinic of the not-all is the one where we find flourishing the pathologies described as centred on the relation to the mother or on narcissism. When we disposed of the previous hierarchy, these were attributed to the pre-Oedipal register, but have now in a way become independent. To call them pre-Oedipal is obviously too restricted.

When we consider everything of the order of addictions, we can clinically observe the frenzy of the not-all, pathologies where it is precisely the without limits of the series that is highlighted. At the same time we observe the decline in effectiveness of the paternal metaphor and the pluralisation and pulverisation of the S_1s. For some years now, we have recognised the crisis of our classifications. Let us take only the category of perversion, to which we are attached by the teaching that we have received and distributed. It must be said that this is a category that has undergone a massive social rejection. It is assimilated to a stigma. One cannot erase from the category of perversion the fact that it refers to a norm, that it belongs to the previous regime, which was dominated by norms and ideals.

Obviously, we object – Lacan says that perversion is the norm of desire. But it is the very terms in which the diagnosis is posed, the category itself, that have ceased to be operative. On the other hand, Lacan has indicated to us other ways of approaching the contemporary clinic as a clinic of the not-all. He has given us the way of the knot. It is not that the knot is elevating in itself. It is rather that the knot is in fact a way of responding to the structure of the not-all, given that this clinic presents us with an indefinite series of arrangements on the basis of three rings of string. The ternary RSI is distinguished from and opposed to what was the tight, discontinuous repartition between neurosis, perversion and psychosis.

Previously we had a combinatory clinic, centred on the Name of the Father, to put it briefly, whose states were discontinuous, giving us clearly distinguished categories. This is not invalid, but it is obvious that referring clinical practice to the knot undoubtedly gives us arrangements that are different but in continuity with one another. We have lost the security of the discontinuous and the clearly distinct. The result is that the symptom has become the elementary unit of the clinic, rather than what we called clinical structure, which was a class. The symptom has become the elementary unit of the clinic. In the end, the symptom, what Lacan called the *sinthome* at the end of his teaching, is the Lacanian version of the fragmentation of clinical entities in the DSM. It is not the same fragmentation, but it is the same movement of de-structuring of entities that can be observed in Lacan's late clinic.

We first operated with a clinic centred on identification. Lacan's first clinic was a clinic of identification: in analysis I learn to tell my story truthfully, that is to say, I elaborate an identification that allows me to be veridical. The end of the analysis entails the satisfactory development of a new identification, which passes through a disidentification, etc, but the central category is identification. Lacan's second clinic was a clinic centred on the fantasy, that is, still a story, but this time a story conceived as an unconscious scenario centred on the subject's relation to the core of jouissance that fills his constitutive lack.

Well, Lacan's last clinic has the symptom as its pivotal term. In this clinic, the absolute, the substance, is jouissance. To go back to the reference to Spinoza that I introduced at the beginning, it's really *Deus sive natura, sive* jouissance. That is, there is nothing but jouissance, to the detriment of truth and meaning. At this point, it is no longer a question of there being a cure at the end of analysis, nor is it a question of a crossing. It is only a question of the passage from one regime of jouissance to another, from a regime of suffering to a regime of pleasure.

What can be said of psychoanalysts in the era of globalisation can be discovered from the pass. If one sees clearly what the translation of this is in terms of what is being staged by the machine of the not-all, the pass means that we are led to propose a disconnection between being an analyst and the practice of analysis. Those who Lacan wished to consecrate as Analysts of the School had necessarily to be of the School, because this entailed a definition of the analyst independent of analytic practice, trying in this way to solve the problem of preserving the analytic core of the practice in a world where the analyst tends to be dissolved within attentional practice.

It is within this context that we must consider analytic formation. At the same time this turns out to be difficult to determine because from now on we must think it outside of any ideal to be attained, outside the very problematic of the ideal and the norm. This means that formation tends to be grasped more as the communication of a way of life than as access to the realisation of an ideal.

Translated by Alasdair Duncan
Revised by Roger Litten

A Fantasy

Jacques-Alain Miller

A Fantasy
Jacques-Alain Miller

Let me begin with a fantasy, an idea that came to me yesterday morning, while I was listening to our colleagues tell us about just the same thing: contemporary, postmodern or – why not? – hyper-modern subjects are *desinhibidos*, neo-disinhib-ited, *desamparados*, disorientated. I was thinking while listening to them: Oh, yes! Oh, yes, yes, yes! And how much so! How disorientated we are! How true that is! It is rare to see four colleagues, one after the other, so thoroughly in agreement with an another, to find oneself in agreement with them and to have the feeling that everyone agrees with them, that there is a consensus.

Lecture given at the IVth Congress of the World Association of Psychoanalysis, in Comandatuba-Bahia, Brazil, August 2004. Original French text established by Monique Kusnierek and published as "Une Fantaisie" in *Mental 15*, February 2005. [TN: The French title Une Fantaisie and its use in the body of the text translates more precisely as "a flight of fancy" or "a flight of the imagination", even "a whim". It is distinct from "un fantasme", translated usually as "a fantasy".]

The Metaphor of Nature by the Real

I wondered then, while listening to them: but how long has it been so, how long have we all been disorientated? And my answer was: probably since civilised morals, as Freud said, were shaken to their roots, probably since they disintegrated. And it's not as if psychoanalysis counted for nothing in the disintegration of civilised morals.

All of us here – or at least almost all of us, not the younger ones in the audience – remember what those civilised morals were. We are still aware of what they mean. We are at least sufficiently familiar with them to be able to understand and even to feel that the present state of our civilisation is immoral, is moving towards immorality. And in fact, civilised morals, in Freud's sense, were a compass for us. They were a handrail for those in distress to lean on, probably because they were inhibiting.

Just the same, we can wonder why these civilised morals, during the Belle Epoque – towards the end of the second half of the nineteenth century, during the Victorian period that Lacan evoked for us – why these morals were so cruel. Perhaps this moral cruelty was already a response to a crack, a fault in civilisation that was to become wider and wider with time. It might be that these civilised morals, as long as they were alive in people's hearts, had already constituted a reaction formation, as we say, to a process of disorientation that had been going on for a somewhat longer time.

And so, I was daydreaming. Perhaps we have been going around in circles ever since compasses have existed, I mean since agricultural practice – which is not ours, which is not necessarily at the forefront – has little by little given up its dominant position in our industrial societies. We do not think about agriculture enough. Perhaps that is where all the trouble is coming from: from the metaphor that is replacing agriculture with industry. Ah, agricultural civilisation, what a grand thing it was!

Agricultural civilisation finds its bearings through nature, through the invariable cycle of seasons. Of course, there is a history of climate that some well-intentioned people are now reconstituting. But this history changes in no way the invariable cycle of seasons that gave its rhythm to agricultural civilisation, so that, in fact, it was possible to find one's bearings and one's symbols in the seasons and the skies. The agricultural real is celestial; it is a friend of nature. With industry, with what has been called the industrial revolution, all that was swept away, little by little. The artifices were multiplied. And now we are all forced to note that the real is devouring nature, that the real is being substituted for it and is proliferating. Here we have a second metaphor: the metaphor that substitutes the real for nature.

I was also thinking that this is the charm of the Seminar *Anxiety*,[1] which I read more than once after establishing the text. This seminar presents, in effect, *objet petit a* in the state of nature, so to speak. An *objet petit a* that is detached from the body, that is a piece of body – whether one is sensitive or insensitive to this piece of the body – it is an *objet petit a* that is in a state of nature, that is taken at that level. On the other hand, when what is in question is the industrial production of surplus jouissance, if we had to describe that, we would, of course, have to put the accent elsewhere.

A New Compass

So my fantasy continued along these lines, with a question: if we are without a compass, as my friend Jorge said, does that mean we are without a discourse? Does that mean we are chaotic, schizo-phrenic, as Deleuze and Guattari, who were generously discussed this afternoon, proposed? And to begin with, are we really without any compass at all? Perhaps we have another compass.

There is a phrase of Lacan's that was cited twice yesterday and formerly served as my compass

---

1 Lacan, J., *Seminar X, Anxiety*, ed. J.-A. Miller, transl. A.R. Price, Cambridge, Polity Press, 2014.

in the course I did with Éric Laurent on "The Other Which Does Not Exist and Its Ethical Committees". It is the phrase that signals the rise to the social zenith of *objet petit a* – the zenith and the nadir are two locatable points in the sky, the zenith the highest point and the nadir the lowest point. This phrase acted as a compass, for me at least, because it signalled that we had touched the sky. We had touched the antique and immobile sky, the immutable agricultural sky that societies that were immobile or slow to change, societies that were cold or lukewarm, held as their reference. What this phrase of Lacan's signalled was that a new star had risen in the social sky, in the *sociel*[2] – *socielo* in Spanish. And this new *sociel* star, so to speak, is, as Lacan had remarked about *objet petit a*, always the result of a forcing, of a passage beyond limits, which Freud discovered, in his own terms, precisely in a beyond. It is an intensive element that makes any notion of measure obsolete, that goes in the direction of the always more, that goes towards the measureless, following a cycle that is not the cycle of the seasons, but a cycle of accelerated renewal, of frenetic innovation.

The Hypermodern Discourse of Civilisation

And so, right away, I wondered: might not *objet*

2 [TN: The neologism *sociel* in French plays on 'social', the Spanish '*socielo*' and the word for 'sky' or 'heaven' in French, *ciel*.]

petit a be – how can we put it? – the compass of civilisation today? And why not? Let's try to see what the principle of the hypermodern discourse of civilisation is. Let's see if we can construct this discourse.

In this possible discourse of civilisation, we will give this object the dominant place. 'Object' is a debatable denomination for Lacan himself. When he named what was at issue the "correlative object of a subject" (and, what's more, put it within parentheses to be sure it stayed in its place), this designation did not seem totally satisfying to Lacan himself. Anyway, let's use it.

This object – here is our hypothesis – is imposed on the disorientated subject and invites him to get past his inhibitions. I am going to write it, very simply, with the symbol we commonly use, $\math$.

$$a \;\rightarrow\; \math</mathbb{S}>$$

We recently pinpointed the term 'evaluation'. To say we pinpointed it is going too far. Rather, it was imposed on us, we have been pestered by this term; all Europe has been browbeaten by the term 'evaluation', which has already passed into current use, I believe, in the United States of America. Now it is taking a tyrannical path in Europe.

Suppose that the disorientated subject is invited to produce evaluation. I write it then as: S_1

$$a \;\rightarrow\; \underline{\underline{S}}$$
$$S_1$$

What I write as S_1 is the countable One of evaluation, of the evaluation to be produced. It seems to me all the more appropriate because in this place, it is substituted for the S_1 of the master signifier that is, for its part, destined to fall. I could find still other significations for this S_1, for example I could see in it the signifier of what is called, in the United States, 'self help'. I saw that in Spanish they say *autoayuda*. I have no idea how we might say that in French, and I do not have the impression that there exists yet a term in current use. We speak of personal development, but we hesitate in French to translate 'self help', we do not yet dare.

I believe you see what I am getting at in my fantasy: I want to get to where I can write S_2 also in the fourth place. S_2, knowledge in the place of truth/lie, does not seem to me to be out of place today in civilisation. The notion that knowledge is nothing but a *semblant* has attracted a great many followers and puts pressure on us. It is not, properly speaking, a matter of scepticism, or of nihilism, but let's say of a sort of relativism or even, as philosophers sometimes say, of perspectivism

– someone from Argentina testified as to how much he had been relieved by adhering to a perspectivist philosophy.

$$\frac{a}{S_2} \;\rightarrow\; \frac{\mathcal{S}}{S_1}$$

This is the fantasy I propose as the structure of the hypermodern discourse of civilisation! This is where my fantasy has taken me! I cannot do otherwise than follow the direction in which I am headed. And this leads me to conceive that the discourse of hypermodern civilisation has the structure of the discourse of the analyst! I am dumbfounded. The result is extremely surprising, for myself to begin with. It is a result that may seem absurd. And, after all, justifying something like that when it arises is, undeniably, a challenge.

Psychoanalysis, Civilisation's Point of Convergence

To begin with, if we think about it carefully, tranquilly, without emotion, Lacan did not hesitate to propose that the discourse of the master had the same structure as the discourse of the unconscious. Now, the discourse of the master can be said to be a social discourse, the discourse of a civilisation that has prevailed since antiquity. So it is not inconceivable, *a priori*, that the discourse of the civilisation of today might have the same structure as the discourse of the analyst. It is not inconceivable on the more or less desiring foundations from which we work.

But if we accept this, we see where the difficulty lies. The discourse of the analyst was formerly the analyser of the discourse of the unconscious, which was its other side – what Lacan calls the other side of psychoanalysis is the discourse of the master. The discourse of the analyst could thus analyse the discourse of the unconscious. Its interpretative and subversive power was able, in the same stroke, to exert a hold over civilisation and the phenomena of society that it had to deal with, and that we have had to deal with as well, as Lacan tried to show, since the very beginnings of antiquity.

Today, if this fantasy is true, if this fantasy leads somewhere – and that remains to be seen – the discourse of civilisation is no longer the other side of psychoanalysis, it is the accomplishment of psychoanalysis. Bravo! Well played, Papa Freud! But, in that case, it calls into question both the means of psychoanalysis, that is to say, interpretation, and its end, or even its beginning. And we could say – if we consider that the relation between civilisation and psychoanalysis is no longer a relation of one side to the other side – we could say that this concerns rather the relation of convergence, that is to say that each of these four terms remains disjoined from the others within civilisation. On the one hand, the surplus jouissance commands; on the other, the subject works; and on again another, identifications fall and are replaced by the homogenous evaluation of capacities; and this while knowledge of different sorts is busy telling lies and yet makes headway nonetheless. We might say that, in civilisation, these different elements are scattered and that it is only in psychoanalysis, in pure psychoanalysis, that these terms are organised into a discourse. That would make psychoanalysis the point of convergence, the focal point of civilisation. In that case, we can only say "poor civilisation"!

Freudian Fundamentalists and Nostalgia for the Past

This fantasy has at least the advantage of explaining the retreat of certain analysts into the old-school discourse of the master that we used to rely on, their nostalgia for the Name of the Father that Nepomiachi rejected yesterday at the end of his paper – none of that for me, he said. It was no less than a testimony in the guise of a negation that, indeed, there is undoubtedly an appeal for us on the side of a retreat into the discourse of the master. In France, at the very least, there is no lack of psychoanalysts who are preoccupied with that, who dream and busy themselves with the idea of putting the order of the discourse of the master back in place, and they are undoubtedly more numerous than we are. Put the master back in its place in order to be subversive once more: "People of France, yet another effort to be reactionaries, otherwise you will no longer be revolutionaries!" In a text that appeared two or three months ago, we could see sketched out the notion of a reactionary practice of psychoanalysis, in which psychoanalysis would, from now on, consist in passing on to the legendary disorientated subjects the master signifiers of tradition. The author explains that today, the psychoanalyst, who is dealing with these disorientated persons, must really give up his former subversion in order to begin to re-establish for his patient the signifiers of tradition, to put them into his hand, into his head, without which nothing could happen. I am far from having read a great many things in the field of psychoanalysis today, but I have the impression, for the moment in any case, that this has not yet taken on a massive form, but that it is beginning to take shape. And perhaps tomorrow we will have a type of psychoanalysis whose objective will be to reconstitute daddy's unconscious. Moreover, in its principle, this psychoanalytic reaction is no different from the principle behind the rise of fundamentalisms. The notion is the same. We are going to see psychoanalysts reconstituting the unconscious, trying to artificially reconstitute daddy's unconscious, yesterday's unconscious, just as we see the zealots of God taking their place on the stage of the world and changing our daily life, our voyages and our leisure activities. There is no difference: they are Freudian fundamentalists...

A second position is taking shape in psychoanalysis, a position that could be called nostalgic and which consists in holding the position that nothing is happening, nothing is taking place. The unconscious is eternal, listen to the eternal, who is your God, so to speak.

A Neuro-Cognitivist Translation of Metapsychology

And, it seems to me, there is a third position, one that is just taking form – if the first is turned towards the past and the second resides in an eternal present, we can say of this third that it is progressivist. It is the position that was presented yesterday by Agnès Aflalo and Éric Laurent, who did not, of course, assume it as their own. This progressivist position consists in bringing, or trying to bring, psychoanalysis into step with the progress of the sciences and false sciences, of regimenting, recruiting [enrégimenter] psychoanalysis in accordance with such progress. This attempt is not absurd. Moreover, it was not presented to us as such. It is not unprecedented either. Thus, it could be said that Lacan undertook a logical-linguistic translation of Freud's metapsychology, which towards the middle of the twentieth century was showing signs of weakening. Lacan, himself, recognised that he had to use this means in order to breathe new life into psychoanalysis. So, in effect, it is not absurd, *a priori*, to try to give a neuro-cognitivist translation to metapsychology. We might say that it must be judged by its results – Jorge Forbes finds that I am exaggerating, which is quite possible. I am giving proof, then, of an open-mindedness that I can only be congratulated for. I mean that we must not insult the future. We, ourselves, took some time to realise that there was an enormous reflexive industry that had been put into place in the last ten, fifteen, or even, as Agnès Aflalo has informed us, twenty years. For twenty years there have been industrious bees producing this honey: translating metapsychology into neuro-cognitivist terms. And, it must be said, we were completely oblivious until it was already in place on the scene and was beginning, here and there, to cause ructions and disorder. I am in favour of having those who can interest themselves in these issues go out there and bring back news of what is going on.

So, these three positions that I have distinguished seem to me to open onto practices having recourse to suggestion.

The Principle of 'It Works'

The first of these, the reactionary practice of psychoanalysis, proceeds by exalting the symbolic conveyed by tradition. What's more, we are witnessing astounding alliances with all the traditionalisms, which reveal a striking convergence between the Bible and *The Interpretation of Dreams* – unquestionable. The second practice, which I called nostalgic, proceeds by way of consolidating an imaginary refuge. As for the third, which is already, probably, the most advanced, it is dedicated to, devoted to, a rallying, and it rallies on the side of the real of science – or so it thinks.

I have thus distributed the three terms of the symbolic, the imaginary and the real among these three practices. It seems to me that what the three practices have in common is what we abbreviate when we write: $S_1 \rightarrow S_2$, with an arrow between the two terms, that is, the relation between command and execution or between stimulus and response. This means that what these practices, however different they may be, target might be stated in the following terms: in every case, it works.

And then there is the Lacanian practice – or, rather, there will be – because this is about inventing it. Of course, it is not about inventing it ex nihilo. It is about inventing it in the direction that the last Lacan, in particular, opened up. And we can probably intuit what this Lacanian practice will be from what stirs us, what spurs us on.

The first thing necessary for this fourth practice, the Lacanian practice of the future, to hold its own, to remain differentiated from the forms I have stigmatised, is to clearly distinguish its principle from the principle of the three other practices, from the principle of 'it works'. Well, Lacanian practice can only have as its principle, if it is to be distinguished from the others, that of 'it fails'. Lacanian practice fails. You recognise moreover, in this failing, a leitmotif of the last Lacan. He did everything he could to place himself in a position to fail with the knots. Obviously, this failing is not a contingent failing. This failing is the manifestation of the relation to an impossible. Incidentally, Lacan was brought to this failing by the indication of Freud himself – psychoanalysis, an impossible profession. And in effect, we, his auditors and readers, have been invaded by these notions of failing and of the impossible. He inoculated us with these terms, which very specifically protected us, which were like antibodies against the discourse of 'it works' and against the new practices of psychoanalysis, all of which have this as their principle. Lacanian practice excludes the notion of success. I will go so far as to say that.

The Law of Failing

I see grimaces, discouragement... Not at all. The objection, obviously, would be: but then Lacanian practice has no value. I do remind you that Lacan did not back off from that. He even ended one of his last lessons in an enigmatic way by saying: "it may be that psychoanalysis is a worthless practice." By the by, you might have noted, at least in France and in Europe, that in all the therapy bench tests, psychoanalysis comes in well and truly last. For psychoanalysts, the fact that we are no better than the others, this then engenders a feeling of guilt. But we too, we tell ourselves, do have our successes. Of course, of course! But we should perhaps not be too proud of these successes either, because they belong to such a contingency that they do not invalidate the law of failing. Rather they are its demonstration. Of course, we have the pass! Some succeed. But they are, precisely, so few that it is obvious it is only to persuade the others that they have failed in their analysis! Obviously this logic is somewhat peculiar, and Lacan once gave us an indication that I took up myself some time ago. It is a logic in which contingency proves, or at least attests to, the impossible. Fundamentally, the fact that contingency exists means that we cannot even say that failing is the law of the real, but, according to Lacan's enigmatic formula, that the real is lawless. If there were no contingency to belie the impossible, we would have law in the real. We do not even have that.

Let's come back to our discourse of civilisation. How can we understand the first line of the discourse of hypermodern civilisation? What meaning can we give to this matheme which is so familiar to us, what meaning can we give it when, contrary to appearances, what we have is not the discourse of the analyst, but the discourse of civilisation?

Surplus jouissance has risen up to the dominant place. Now, surplus jouissance is correlative to what I would call, to speak like A. R. Damasio – I am cultivating myself – a state of the body proper and, as such, surplus jouissance is asexuated. It commands – but what does it command? It does not command an 'it works', but an 'it fails', which we write, precisely, $\mathcal{S}$. When we bar a letter, it is generally because we have made an error. Here, the surplus jouissance commands an 'it fails' and precisely an 'it fails' in the sexual order. And I do not see what prevents our considering that this $ writes: there is no sexual rapport, and so much the more so as the initial letter, S, is the same as the initial of sex. This would lead us to say that the non-existence of the sexual relation has precisely, today, become obvious to the point that it can be made explicit, written, from the moment that the *objet petit a* rose to the *sociel*.

In the regime of the discourse of the master, on the other hand, the sexual rapport was a truth repressed by the master signifier. But we are well obliged to take note that today the master signifier, master signifiers no longer manage to give any existence to the sexual rapport. That brings on the despair of the religious, except for those who precisely keep their distance from hypermodern civilisation and who defend with talent and with vigour an older form, a traditional form – indeed, today, a meritorious resistance to the *objet petit a* is being exercised by the Islamic side of civilisation. In hypermodern societies, on the contrary, religion is in despair on this point, sex is a source of despair for it – it is still the sexual question that slows down the rise and the comeback of religion, in the way that a Christian, Catholic sociologist I have read has explained. And if, among hypermodern societies, religion despairs on this point, it is because religion, for us, leans on a notion of nature that the real has outdated, that the rise of the *objet petit a* has rendered obsolete.

Obviously, what can make us burst into laughter or tears is the fact that a great number of psychoanalysts have no better idea than to reinforce this. They swear in the name of their experience that the education of children requires them to make their identifications with mummy and daddy. I consider this to be an abuse. An abuse that cannot possibly be established from their experience. It was already ridiculous when they turned themselves into the guardians of collective reality, but it is all the more ridiculous when the collective reality whose guardians they want to be is that of yesterday. To say this implies no enthusiasm whatsoever for the readjustments that are under way. As for most of you, I was educated in an old, more traditional way, but I do follow what is being written.

Psychoanalysis was invented to respond to a discontent in civilisation, a subjective discontent, we might say, that of a subject plunged into a civilisation that could be stated like this: in order to give existence to the sexual relation, jouissance must be restrained, inhibited, repressed. Freudian practice paved the way to what was demonstrated – with all the quotation marks you want – as a liberation of jouissance. Freudian practice anticipated the rise of the *objet petit a* to the social zenith and this practice contributed to its installation. Besides, this *objet petit a* is not a star, it is a Sputnik – an artificial product.

As for Lacanian practice, it has to deal with the consequences of this sensational success. Consequences that are felt to be of the order of a catastrophe. The dictatorship of surplus jou-issance is devastating nature, it is fragmenting marriage, dispersing the family and remodelling the body. This remodelling does not only concern plastic surgery or dieting – the anorexic lifestyle, as Dominique Laurent was saying – it can go as far as more major surgery and other operations on the body. Now that the genome has been deci-phered, decrypted, it is really going to be possible to advance towards what some authors have called post-humanity.

So is Lacanian practice playing its part in rela-tion to the practice and standards of the IPA? Very probably. But it is above all playing its part in rela-tion to the new reals that the discourse of hyper-modern civilisation gives evidence of. It is playing its part in the dimension of a real that fails, in such a way that the relation between the two sexes is going to become more and more impossible, in such a way that, if I may say so, the one-all-alone will be the post-human standard, the one-all-alone, all alone to fill out questionnaires in order to receive one's evaluation, and the one-all-alone commanded by a surplus-jouissance that is pre-sented under its most anxiety-provoking aspect.

A Hole of the Real
Thus, Lacanian practice, which is to be invented, will not operate with reference to the discourse of

the unconscious as its other side. It will operate, it is already operating through us – let us try to find our bearings – it is operating in a hole of the real that works, and a hole is not a lack – lack is always in its place, lack is the other name for place. Lack is the principle of all substitutions and it is even what permits us to say at a given moment: Bingo! On the contrary, Lacanian practice operates in the dimension of a failing. We also say Bingo! in Lacanian practice. It is a miracle, a grace. But it must be recognised, as Lacan himself did, that it cannot be calculated. Analytic interpretation, to the extent that we understand how it proceeds, is not an analytic interpretation. That is how I understand the fact that Lacan took us by the hand, finally, in order to reassure us that there is nothing but different ways to fail, some more satisfying than others. We are not simply playing on words here, with witticisms, it is not simply a *Witz*. This is the condition under which we will hold our own in the discourse of hypermodern civilisation.

So this Lacanian practice would be the form, the deformation and the transformation, in the topological sense, that might permit psychoanalysis to overcome the real consequences that are occurring as a result of a century of its exercise, as a result of its introduction into a civilisation that is now converging on the structure of analytic discourse. And these consequences make psychoanalysis reflect back on psychoanalysis itself. The consequences of psychoanalysis make psychoanalysis reflect back on itself and, on this path, we can even say that what was once its condition of possibility is becoming a condition of impossibility. I say possibility, but it is rather a matter of the contingency of the Freud event, and it might be that that impossibility, which had already been stated by Freud and which has been articulated by Lacan, is the condition of the very exercise of psychoanalysis. In any case, this is what has become clear for us, not intellectually, but in practice: psychoanalysis *ex-sists* with an impossible as its basis. Moreover, we note that we have lost the taste for telling each other about our therapeutic successes. It is rather when we testify to a stumbling block that we have the feeling that it is true – which Mauricio Mazzotti, for example, understood very well yesterday when he related an interpretation that missed its mark, a failing in his practice that was much more appreciated than it would have been for the euphoric narration of a presentation such as "I pushed on this button, I got this result and the mask fell." This is precisely because we do not understand how interpretation functions, because success is not obtained by pushing buttons, whatever the perfection of the diagnosis or of the clinical experience. It is precisely for this reason that we spend our time explaining to each other, trying to explain to each other what happened.

Psychoanalysis – which is, if I may say so, a Socratism with a strain of cynicism – has shaken all the *semblants* on which discourses and practices reposed. It thus unveiled what Lacan called the economy of jouissance. Well, now, derision and cynicism have passed into the *sociel*, with just the right amount of the humanitarian necessary to conceal what it concerns. And this propagation of derision has not spared psychoanalysis itself. Psychoanalysis notes today that it is the victim of psychoanalysis. And psychoanalysts are themselves, potentially, victims of psychoanalysis, victims of the suspicion that psychoanalysis instills and distills when they do not manage to believe in the unconscious. The *semblants* by which psychoanalysis was itself produced – the father, Oedipus, castration, the drive, etc – have also begun to tremble. That is why, for twenty years, we have been witness to the recourse to the discourse of science, which we hope will give us the real that is in question, which we hope will be able to give us some surplus jouissance, and which we hope will get us past the barrier that separates S_2 from *petit a* in the discourse of hysteria.

An Intention of Meaning in the Real

I need now to recall the condition of contingency under which psychoanalysis appeared, specifically Freud's discovery of the hysterical symptom, which was made in the context of the discourse of science, of the psycho-physiological materialism at the end of the nineteenth century, in the context of a real in the scientific sense, of a real of the Galilean type, of a real One, lodging, and including, a knowledge. It is in this context that Freud discovered that there is meaning in the real. This, we know, caused a scandal and psychoanalysis appeared to be a corruption of scientific knowledge, because scientific knowledge can be in the real, but in order to have nothing to say.

That there is meaning in the real implies that the real means something, that it has an intention. And that was, for psychoanalysis, its condition of possibility. The meaning in the real is what supports the being of the symptom, in the analytic sense. And yet what Freud was doing was tolerated. We might wonder why. What Freud and his disciples, who began to proliferate, were doing was tolerated. They were allowed to tamper with the symptom, the mental symptom, they were allowed to contaminate it with meaning. It was even tolerated that psychiatry be won over to it. No doubt because they did not have the knowledge in the real that could give a response to symptoms of this kind, except for a crude response: they had lobotomy or the sleeping cure. So the intention of meaning that Freud attributed to the real was tolerated. The treatment of the symptom was left to the manipulation of meaning. Moreover, at least since Pinel, the imperative sense [*sens*], the S_1, had already been in use for the treatment of the symptom, it was traditional.

A Scission Between Meaning and the Real

The Freudian S_2 was thus accepted, that is to say the associative meaning, in addition to the imperative sense. And this up to the present day, when, in order to add, so to speak, to the discontent in psychoanalysis, there occurred a scission in the being of the symptom, or more exactly a scission between the real and meaning. But this scission was expected, logically expected. The result is the pulverisation of the symptom, which is testified to by the successive editions of the DSM, after the first edition, which was psychodynamic. What permitted the symptom to hold together was the act (or fact) of saying [*le dire*]. The symptom had something to say. It was, ultimately, the unconscious intentionality that held the symptom together. Well! in the word symptom, the "sym" has gone away and all that is left is the "ptom"! The symptom is from now on reduced to the trouble.

And English says that better when it speaks of "disorder", a word that takes its reference from the order of the real.

For science, the real is what works. And that is what the knowledge in the real is for. That is why we can say that science has affinities with the discourse of the master – which Lacan pointed out a thousand times, moreover. But in hypermodern civilisation, no one believes this any more. On the contrary, we now have the idea that scientific knowledge, in the real, fails, that it is going to fail. Genetically modified organisms, nuclear technology, none of this generates confidence any more in the correct functioning of knowledge in the real – and this was so, of course, from the moment we began to tamper with it.

What used to be the symptom, and which is now nothing but a trouble, is from now on divided in two, doubled. On the side of the real, it is treated as outside-meaning [*hors-sens*], by biochemistry, by medication that is more and more precisely targeted. And on the side of meaning, it continues to exist as a residue. It is the object of an adjunct treatment, which essentially can take two forms, it seems to me. On the one hand, we have a practice of listening that is pure semblance – "come here so I can listen to you" – which has a value of accompaniment and often even a value of control over the operation that is accomplished in the real by the use of medication – and, indeed, the biochemists are the first to say: "but not at all, our patients also need to be listened to." On the other hand, we have the practice of authoritarian and protocolary speech in cognitive behavioural therapies.

The symptom finds itself, then, divided in two. On the side of the real, the aim is the more or less approximative suppression of the trouble; and on the side of meaning, we find a welcoming of meaning, a flowing of meaning and, at the same time, a levelling out of meaning. It is especially on the side of the cognitive behavioural therapies that we find a refusal, a refutation of the symptom, while in psychoanalysis, the symptom used to have a value of truth, it represented the truth, always presenting it behind a mask, and so as a lie, and it was necessary to take the time to verify the symptom, "verify" in the sense of rendering it true. Today, we see that in France, the time that it is necessary to take is no longer a matter of course.

How can we respond to that?

Firstly, we have a psychoanalytic protest that has its appeal, but is futile, and which consists in impugning the knowledge in the real. Secondly, we have what I called a rallying of knowledge in the real. Thirdly, we have the attempt to renovate the meaning of the symptom, which Lacan set out to do. This is what he introduced by modifying the very spelling of the word symptom, as *sinthome*.

Here we must go back to Freud and his discontent in civilisation, which was not simply a diagnosis, but a support for psychoanalysis, its promise of success. Today, I am taking as a reference, rather, the outline he gave in 1908, under the title *"Die 'kulturelle' Sexualmoral und die moderne Nervosität"* ("Civilised" Sexual Morality and Modern Nervous Illness"). It is a text that is amusing to re-read and it is not very long. Freud cites in it all the observers of the time, who at the turn of the century, between the nineteenth and twentieth centuries, took note of the new symptoms that were marking this turning point – the most celebrated, which has remained with us, being Beard's neurasthenia. All the observers noted one social phenomenon: the growth and proliferation of nervous illness. This passage is very amusing and down to earth; it gives a description of modern life, of the fatigue that it implies, and of over-stimulation. We could really believe it was talking about today. What is striking is that Freud quotes all that at the beginning of his text, only to then put it aside and extract, on the contrary, one unique factor, one essential determinant: monogamy, the monogamous exigency. This is how he swiftly sketches a theory of sexual jouissance in civilisation. First step: free access to jouissance – that really is, as Jean-Jacques Rousseau says:

"let us dispense with the facts." Second step: the restriction of jouissance, which is only permitted for reproductive ends. And thirdly, jouissance, today, is only permitted as part of monogamous marriage. It is amusing to follow this text in detail. Freud isolates what causes neurosis by considering the effort to make the sexual relation exist and the sacrifice of jouissance that that entails. We find there the finger pointing to what Lacan's contribution will be.

Symptoms of the Sexual Non-Rapport

Lacan's contribution does not consist at all in contesting the scientific real and knowledge in the real. Contesting the discourse of science is a path to perdition, which opens the way to all the finagling of the psy – 'finagling' is not an insulting term. It is not a question of contesting this knowledge, but of admitting that there is knowledge in the real and, at the same time, positing that in this knowledge there is a hole, that sexuality makes a hole in this knowledge. This is a transformation of Freud, probably, and it means forming a new alliance between science and psychoanalysis that rests on the non-relation.

"There is no sexual rapport" gives us, then, the site of Lacanian practice, because it must be heard in light of the statement that asserts "there is knowledge in the real." "There is no sexual rapport" is the counterweight to "there is knowledge in the real." It is the sexual rapport that objects to the omnipotence of the discourse of science – moreover, for the moment, marriage bureaux are left in the hands of a certain number of matrons who have experience with this. The evaluators have not yet taken over the marriage bureaux, but they will not be long in coming! So, for the moment, and this is what is, all the same, striking, the sexual rapport makes a hole in the real and in the knowledge in the real.

That the sexual rapport makes a hole in the real can be expressed simply like this: the software fails at this point. This is the principle of a practice or of a clinic in which the symptoms are not troubles or disorders, because at that point there is no order. That means that the knowledge in the real does not dictate its law and we cannot intervene at that point starting from the knowledge in the real. This is a negative statement that calls for positive statements, and I will have to make a choice, because I am at the end of my talk.

First, symptoms are symptoms of the sexual non-rapport. This means that they are no doubt articulated into signifiers, but that is secondary, it is their chitter-chatter. Symptoms are not essentially messages. They are above all signs of the sexual non-rapport, possibly punctuation marks. Lacan spoke of symptoms as question marks in the sexual non-rapport. Yesterday, I heard a patient say that what remained for her of anxiety was linked to her body like a comma, like a pause in respiration. So, symptoms are signs. That is an approach other than the one that treats them as messages.

Symptoms Are Real

On the other hand, symptoms are necessary. They do not cease to be written, and this is what founds their equivalence with the etcetera. This means they are real to such an extent that they can very easily be confused with the real that works. There lies the paradox. This is why, at the same time that Lacan says the symptom is real, he can also say: we must believe in it. As a matter of fact, they are so real, these symptoms, that it is arbitrary to detach them as such – someone has to really want to. Would you like an example? Take homosexuality. It was posited as a trouble within the natural order. When you contend that a trouble of being is a trouble of the natural order, there is, today, only one thing to be done: you must form a lobby. And if you form a lobby, the outcome is that you no longer are a trouble of the natural order. As you know, it was as a result of pressure, of a balance of political power, that homosexuality came to no longer be considered as a disorder, or classified as a disorder. We can see here, therefore, the extent to which this is in accordance with the results of psychoanalysis, of a particular psychoanalysis, namely: perverse jouissance is permitted. The question is what one does with it.

A third positive statement: symptoms are jouissance-symptoms, so to speak. What they express is that jouissance is not at the place where we thought it should be, that is to say, in the sexual rapport that Freud gives us a caricature of, in the guise of monogamy. We never have the right jouissance, the one that there should be. And, from there, we access a certain number of knot-points of this clinic, which I am not going to tell you about today and which involve questions. The incorporation of the unconscious, and is the unconscious corporeal? Lacanian practice and Lacan's oh-so-troubling question on practice: does the effect of interpretation come from the use of words or from their jaculation? Which is to say that for an interpretation, you have to find the tone – moreover those who have the chance to be able to relate some of Lacan's interpretations always repeat them using Lacan's tone. The poetics of interpretation is not there for its aesthetics, it is not there to be kitsch. The poetics of interpretation is a materialism of interpretation. Someone who has been following a patient for nine years told me yesterday, or the day before yesterday, during her supervision, that she had obtained an effect unlike any other she had obtained during the nine previous years simply by saying: *Basta*!, in a tone whose virulence contrasted drastically with the usual soft tone of her voice. One must, then, bring one's body into play in order for the interpretation to be raised to the power of the symptom.

I am looking for a point of suspension, not of conclusion.

Love, Which Makes the Unconscious Exist

With the last Lacan, we find ourselves with three unconsciouses, three different modalities of the unconscious, but we need some time to explain that.

We can say that the Freudian unconscious works until its thirst is quenched [*jusqu'à plus soif*]. What's more, Marco Focchi brought a list of references in which we see the Freudian unconscious work itself to exhaustion, whereas the Lacanian *parlêtre* does not work itself to exhaustion. Rather, it swarms, bubbles up and infects; its style is parasitic. Lacan wanted the Lacanian *parlêtre* to replace the Freudian unconscious. It seems to me that he wanted it to bring a response to the problem that I posed on the blackboard, namely that psychoanalysis must move into fourth gear.

The considerations that I had to skip over would lead us to invert what we say traditionally:

the subject supposed to know is the pivot of transference. It seems to me that the last Lacan says something else, he says rather, if I may put it this way: transference is the pivot of the subject supposed to know. In other words, he says that what makes the unconscious *ex-sist* as knowledge, is love. Moreover, the question of love, starting with the seminar *Encore*, has provoked special interest, because love is what could effect a mediation between the ones-all-alone – and with that in mind, saying that love is imaginary presents some difficulty. This means that the unconscious does not exist. The primary unconscious does not exist as knowledge. For it to become a knowledge, to make it exist as knowledge, love is necessary. And that is why Lacan could say at the end of his seminar *Les non-dupes errent*: a psychoanalysis requires that one love one's unconscious. It is the only way to make the rapport, to establish a rapport between S_1 and S_2, because in the primary state, we have disjoined Ones, we have scattered Ones. So a psychoanalysis requires that one love one's unconscious in order to make, not the sexual rapport, but the symbolic rapport, exist. But a psychoanalyst is not required to love the unconscious. A psychoanalyst is not required to love the effects of truth from the unconscious. And that is difficult, because an analyst is also an analysand or a former analysand. And yet, in the name of what Lacanian practice could be, we must not love the true any more than the beautiful or the good.

Translated by Thelma Sowley
Revised by Michele Julien

**Psychoanalytical
Notebooks**

London Society
of the New
Lacanian School

Individual or institutional online purchases including
iBooks and Kindle versions:

On our website www.londonsociety-nls.org.uk
(Exchange rate at the time of purchase applies)

Single issues from PN33 onwards are £12 plus p&p
(Institutions £15 plus p&p)

A single issue of PN24 onwards is £15 plus p&p
(Institutions £20 plus p&p)

A single issue for previous issues up to PN23 is £10
(Institutions £15 plus p&p)

Postage and packing: UK £2 EU £4 Others £6.00

Please contact us for ongoing subscriptions and
any other questions: janetrhaney@gmail.com

The Psychoanalytical Notebooks can also
be purchased in the following bookshops:

London
Karnac Books
12 New College Parade
Finchley Road
London NW3 5EP

Paris
Librairie de l'ecf
1, rue Huysmans
75006 Paris